Peterbilt

LONG-HAUL LEGEND

J.E. Beach

motorbooks

First published in 2008 by Motorbooks, an imprint of MBI Publishing Company, 400 First Avenue North, Suite 300, Minneapolis, MN 55401 USA

Motorbooks titles are also available at discounts in bulk quantity for industrial or sales-promotional use. For details write to Special Sales Manager at MBI Publishing Company, 400 First Avenue North, Suite 300, Minneapolis, MN 55401 USA.

To find out more about our books, join us online at www. motorbooks.com.

Library of Congress Cataloging-in-Publication Data

Beach, James, 1953–
  Peterbilt : long-haul legend / James Beach.
    p. cm.
  Includes index.
  ISBN 978-0-7603-3269-6 (hb w/ jkt)
  1. Peterbilt trucks—History. 2. Tractor trailer combinations—United States—History. I. Title.
  TL230.5.P48B43 2008
  629.2240973—dc22
                                2008023123

On the cover: This 2001 Peterbilt Model 379, dubbed *Dead Man's Hand*, features design elements reflecting the poker hand supposedly held by Wild Bill Hickok when he was fatally shot while playing cards in a saloon in Deadwood, South Dakota (known then as the Dakota Territory). The truck was rebuilt and customized by Outlaw Customs of Henderson, Colorado. *Paul Hartley*

On the frontispiece: An old-style nameplate makes an appearance on this Model 379's hood to reinforce the truck's nickname as *Tired Iron.*

On the title pages: This 1994 Peterbilt 379, owned by James Davis of Medford, Oregon, illustrates that even a 13-year old truck can still look great and work hard. It also shows the level of customization owners can add to their trucks to make each Peterbilt Model 379 as different as its owner.

On the back cover, top left: Teresi Trucking's 1948 Model 270 DD was originally a singledrive-axle truck, but a second drive was added somewhere along the line. The restored truck includes upgrades in several areas, including the interior. It's been a restored beauty almost as long as it was a working truck. Teresi Trucking of Lodi, California, restored the classic in the early 1970s and still uses it in shows and other truck events. **Top right:** Peterbilt's aerodynamic models, such as this Model 387, have become popular fleet options and compete with other aerodynamic trucks for fleet business. **Bottom:** This 1967 Model 358 dump owned by Phil's Trucking of Gardnerville, Nevada, is an example of one of Peterbilt's first tilt-hood models.

Editor: Amy Glaser
Designer: Mandy Iverson

Printed in China

Contents

Foreword

After writing about the trucking industry for the last 20 years, I'm quite confident in saying that all commercial truck makers produce quality vehicles. These trucks are technologically advanced, aerodynamic, comfortable, reliable, and durable. Today's heavy trucks are more durable, easier to operate, and more comfortable than trucks produced just 20 years ago. There is no doubt that the trucks built 20 years from now will surpass today's models in every facet.

The various truck makers all have loyal customers, and some of these manufacturers command a larger share of the U.S. Class 8 truck market each year. On the other hand, there is no denying that truckers consider Peterbilts to be special. Truck driver surveys consistently show that Peterbilt is ranked number one as the truck that drivers prefer to drive or would like to drive. Companies that use them swear their trucks help attract and keep drivers. Customizing shops have a huge business selling chrome and stainless-steel parts, lights, and other upgrades for Peterbilts. It is by far the dominant truck driven by truckers that participate in the truck show circuit. Show up at any truck beauty contest and 80 to 90 percent of the entries will be Peterbilts.

Even in an era of sky-rocketing fuel prices, Peterbilt's long-nose traditional trucks are very popular with owner-operators. For these truckers—small business people who really understand their business—any aerodynamic penalty is offset by what a Peterbilt says about their business. "It sends a message when I pull into a shipper's terminal in this truck," said a trucker when referring to his immaculate, customized Peterbilt Model 379. "It says I'm serious about what I do."

Peterbilt's legacy is due in large part to the success the company has had in targeting such owner-operators with its flagship products such as the Model 379 or its predecessor Model 359. Its work trucks are legends in their own rights, but in many ways, Peterbilt's emergence as a long-haul trucking icon is tied to the success independent truckers have had in carving out a niche for themselves in a very competitive and tough trucking industry.

Acknowledgments

When you write a book about a brand like Peterbilt, you are not sailing off into uncharted waters. Millions of words, dozens of books, countless magazine articles, songs, and websites have explored the subject of Peterbilt trucks. This vast amount of information available on Peterbilt trucks attests to a long-standing interest from truck drivers, fleet owners, and vintage-truck enthusiasts. Peterbilt enthusiasts know their Petes, as demonstrated by a comment I saw on a website for fans of the movie *Texas Chainsaw Massacre*. Someone had posted a question about the semi-truck shown in the movie. A response from another poster not only identified the truck as a Peterbilt Model 351, but then went on to explain why it was probably a 1961 model year 351. The respondent gleaned this from watching the scene a couple of times.

The company's history is recounted not only on Peterbilt's website, but in a number of books and articles, many of which I turned to for frequent guidance while preparing this latest entry into the Peterbilt canon. The true trailblazers on the subject of Peterbilt include Ronald Adams' *Peterbilt Trucks 1939–1979: At Work*, Henry Rasmussen's *Peterbilt: The Class of the Industry*, and Warren Johnson's *Peterbilt: the Evolution of Class*. Ron Adams supplied several of the old photographs. *The History of the J. G. Brill Co.*, by Debra Brill, provided insights into the Brill Company's investment in Peterbilt's predecessor company Fageol Motor Co. Articles on the Interstate Highway System prepared by the Department of Transportation to commemorate the system's 50th anniversary in 2004 also provided valuable insight into the early years of freight movement. Attributions to other sources can be found within the text.

A large portion of the material covering the last 20 years comes from notes, articles, pictures, and other materials I've collected during that time as a member of the trucking trade press. These came from one-on-one interviews with company executives, plant tours, product demonstrations, press conferences, and scores of trade shows and exhibitions. I've met dozens of Peterbilt employees during this time, from general managers to public relations directors, engineers to dealers. I can't say enough about these hard-working men and women who all were just as passionate as their customers about their products.

Another key source for this book came from the Peterbilt owners I've had the privilege of speaking with over the years; especially the participants in the Stars & Stripes Truck Show events I came to know. I want to thank them for allowing me to take pictures of their trucks and for answering my questions. Members of the Stars & Stripes staff were also extremely helpful.

The American Truck Historical Society and many of its members also provided helpful information and direction. Thanks also to Western States Peterbilt in Sacramento and Courtland Truck Works in Courtland, California. Ed Rocha of Rocha Valley Enterprises in Oakdale, California, and John and Anthony Teresi of Teresi Trucking in Lodi, California, let me take pictures of their restored Peterbilts and use some of their old photographs.

AN ICON RETIRES

The last Peterbilt Model 379 rolled off the assembly line at Peterbilt Motors' Denton, Texas, truck plant on April 4, 2007, as its new owners, Kevin and Laurie Hagenow, watched. With that, an era came to a close for one of America's most popular and iconic truck models. Only 1,000 Model 379 Legacy Class Edition trucks were built, and the Hagenows, owners of TWX Corporation of Two Rivers, Wisconsin, got the last one.

This 1994 Peterbilt 379, owned by James Davis of Medford, Oregon, illustrates that even a 13-year-old truck can still look great and work hard. It also shows the level of customization owners can add to their trucks to make each Peterbilt Model 379 as different as its owner.

Page 8: Peterbilt Model 379s, such as the 2001 *Dead Man's Hand*, often serve as a way for their owners to an artistic vision in chrome accessories and custom paint. This masterpiece was rebuilt and customized from a wreck by Colorado-based Outlaw Customs and proves that even a wrecked Pete can live again. Peterbilt retired the Model 379 in 2007, but it's certain to be well represented on the nation's highways for years to come. *Paul Hartley*

Versatility has always been a hallmark of the Peterbilt brand, and the Model 379 can be found in all types of applications. In its 20-year production run, the truck has come to personify the long road and is one of the true long-haul legends.

According to numerous surveys, truck drivers prefer Peterbilts over any other brand. While Peterbilts are known as owner-operator trucks, many trucking companies prefer the long-nosed, muscular Peterbilts and the image of class they convey. As far as truck beauty shows go, by far the most popular truck on the lot is a Peterbilt 379.

According to Peterbilt press releases, the Hagenows' truck featured some special touches befitting the final model 379, including unique exterior Legacy Class Edition emblems on the grille and both sides of the cab; a custom dash plate inscribed with the number *1,000*; a polished aluminum hood centerline; premium UltraRide seats embroidered with the Legacy Class Edition emblem; a Platinum Oval package, including a punched oval-pattern grille and air cleaner intake screen, polished grille bars, and stainless-steel sun visor; a premium-level interior; ConcertClass surround system with Sirius satellite radio; and a Peterbilt in-dash GPS navigation system.

As the last 379 rolled off the line, its successor, the Model 389 was set to take its place as the company's

In a press release accompanying the event, Kevin Hagenow said, "We are proud to have been chosen to receive this historical truck. It joins our Peterbilt-only fleet and will continue the quality and class image given to each and every customer we service and driver we employ."

The operative word there is *class*. Peterbilt trucks have long been considered the class of America's heavy truck fleet, with Petes featured in songs, movies, and television series over the years. For instance, in the *Transformers* movie released in 2007, Optimus Prime transformed into a modified Model 379.

This 2005 Peterbilt 379, owned by Paul Stanchio of Port Washington, New York, features an extra-long sleeper and works every day hauling cars from the East Coast to the West Coast, and it looks great doing it. Model 379s can be found in all types of trucking applications, from over-the-road carrier to cement mixer to log truck.

next flagship model and begin building its own legend. Incorporating many of the same traditional styling touches of the Model 379—the kind of styling that says "Peterbilt"—the 389 also features improved aerodynamics and incorporates recent technological advances. Despite the new technologies and refined styling touches, the Model 389 remains a Peterbilt through and through, reflecting the models from earlier eras while making its own statement as a long-haul legend.

Chapter 1

HISTORY OF A LEGEND

A number of factors contributed to commercial trucking becoming what it is today—the primary mode of freight transportation in the country in terms of tons moved each year. A trucking executive at an industry event in 2001 said the development of the diesel engine, coupled with advances in road-building techniques and road surfaces, would top his list of such factors. Diesels provide a reliable and powerful source of power, while roads provide the network connecting manufactured goods with their markets.

This 1929 Fageol was part of the private truck collection of A. W. "Pop" Hayes, the founder of the Hayes Antique Truck Museum in Woodland, California. The Fageol was the precursor to Peterbilt trucks. The Fageol trucks sported ventilator louvers that ran front to back along the center of the hood. According to the Hayes Antique Truck Museum, the company held a patent on this design feature, which made Fageol trucks easy to identify. *Courtesy* GO-West *archives*

When the first Peterbilt rolled into service in 1939, the company's predecessor had already been in the truck-building business for more than 20 years, and scores of other manufacturers were cranking out trucks to meet commercial demand, which had jumped sharply following World War I. Prior to the war, railroads and horse-drawn wagons delivered most freight, even though motor trucks were being manufactured and used before that time. According to most sources, the first motor truck was invented by Gottlieb Daimler in 1896. It wasn't long after that motor trucks showed their promise as freight haulers. A story in the March 20, 1910, *The New York Times*

Page 12: Teresi Trucking's 1948 Model 270 DD was originally a single-drive-axle truck, but a second drive was added somewhere along the line. The restored truck includes upgrades in several areas, including the interior. It's been a restored beauty almost as long as it was a working truck. Teresi Trucking of Lodi, California, restored the classic in the early 1970s and still uses it in shows and other truck events.

said, "Motor vehicles will supplant horse-drawn vehicles for business purposes in city and country just as surely as the steam engine supplanted the stage coach in passenger transportation." A. B. Cordner, the writer of the piece, argued, "There is no industry or business in which horses cannot be profitably supplanted by motors."

An article in the January 21, 1912, issue of *The New York Times* describes the events of two recent "motor truck shows." The article described manufacturing and design trends of the time, such as shaft-drive for medium commercial motor wagons and chain-drive for larger ones, the popularity of starting mechanisms, and manufacturers' focus on simple yet foolproof engineering. Some trucks featured the driver's seat above the motor, but the vast majority of models had the driver's seat behind the motor. Even in 1912, truckers preferred conventional trucks over cab-over designs. Some of the heavy motor wagons in 1912 had four speeds, but most had three speeds. Wooden wheels predominated with some cast-steel wheels displayed. Building a truck that can easily accommodate the widest variety of truck bodies and configurations was a challenge faced by early truck makers and remains a challenge for manufacturers today. For truck makers in 1912, that meant building a chassis upon which local wagon makers would mount a body specific for each job and in many cases, each locale.

This 1946 270 is in the process of being restored at Courtland TruckWorks. Darrow Thomson, Jr., the TruckWorks' owner, refers to this vintage as a "hard-nosed Pete." Most of the sheet-metal panels on this truck have been or will be replaced because the original was rusted out. The original cab frame will be reused, and the TruckWorks mechanics fabricated new doors and hood.

Most of the demand for motor trucks in the early days came from merchants in large cities, but trucks were being used in smaller towns, on farms, and in the forests. From the earliest years, motor trucks promised an alternative to the railroads for delivering cargo across the country. A story in the June 16, 1912, *The New York Times* reports that the "first transcontinental delivery in history by a motor truck will soon be made." The delivery entailed hauling three tons of cargo from Philadelphia to Petaluma, California, a 4,436-mile trip. The truck, manufactured by the American Locomotive Company, was a 1910 Alco and featured all-steel construction. The organizers estimated the trip would take 45 days. The five-man crew had to dig the truck out of mud holes

This beautifully restored 1946 Peterbilt, owned and restored by Ed Bonestroo and John Bos, was on display at the Ability First Working Truck Show in Pomona, California, during June 2000.

included a number of light and heavy motor trucks and a variety of cars. The army assigned Lieutenant Colonel Dwight D. Eisenhower to observe the truck train. His report made clear that the country needed adequate roads in order for trucks to be useful in hauling military cargo. His key finding was, "Extended trips by trucks through the middle-western part of the United States are impracticable until roads are improved, and then only a light truck should be used on long hauls." The paved part of the Lincoln Highway, the main cross-country route at the time, ended in Illinois and did not pick up again until California. Many good roads were too narrow for commercial trucks, and in some areas the grades were too steep for trucks to negotiate. The trip reportedly had a huge impact on Eisenhower's promotion of a national highway system when he became president in 1952. A copy of Eisenhower's report can be found on the Federal Highway Administration's website: www.fhwa.dot.gov.

PETERBILT'S FORERUNNER

As demand for commercial trucks continued to rise in the early 1900s, a number of regional truck makers sprang up to meet that demand. One such company was Fageol Motors Company, which began producing tractors, buses, and automobiles in Oakland, California, in 1916. The Fageol brothers had distributed automobiles and trucks, such as the Rambler and Garford, for the Thomas B. Jeffery Company for a number of years before opening their factory. Charles Nash bought the Jeffery company and prompted the formation of the Fageol Motors Company.

and move rocks out of the way; they had to blaze their own trail in many areas to make the trip. The hardships encountered along the way made it clear that hauling cargo by motor truck required good roads.

Trucks saw their first military use during World War I. After the war, the military continued to test trucks for their value in moving cargo and troops. In 1919, a transcontinental truck train made the trip from Washington, D.C., to California. The truck train

The company soon began making trucks to meet the rising demand for rugged, reliable commercial trucks designed for the tough operational environment, such as the vast deserts and steep mountain passes that existed in the western United States. Fageol trucks became popular with farmers and loggers and were used by a number of the early western trucking companies, such as Consolidated Freight Lines.

Almost from the beginning, Fageol Motors established a relationship with the Hall-Scott Company of Berkeley, California. Hall-Scott was formed by Elbert John Hall and Bert C. Scott to build engines for automobiles. The company soon expanded its line to include engines for trucks, rail cars, and airplanes. An automobile was the first Fageol vehicle to include a Hall-Scott engine. Fageol buses were also powered by Hall-Scott.

The year the Fageol brothers incorporated their company in California, 1916, was the same year the Lincoln Highway was finished. The new highway ran through Oakland, California, along several existing city streets, including Foothill Boulevard. The Fageol factory was on this street and established an early link between the trucks that would become Peterbilts and transcontinental highways. Fageol was well known for its buses and bus chassis during this time, and a number of bus lines used Fageol buses in their fleets, including Peerless Stages of Oakland.

According to some published accounts, the Fageol name was originally known for producing farm tractors. The demand for trucks created by World War I prompted the company to focus more on motor trucks than tractors. In an article that appeared in the May/June 1996 issue of *Polk's Antique Tractor Magazine*, author Bill Vossler wrote that if not for the war, Fageol may have become the most popular name in farm tractors instead of being the forerunner to the most popular name in heavy trucks. The company quit making orchard tractors during an agricultural

slowdown in 1923. Putting all its energies into trucks and buses, the company grew.

The success of the company's buses prompted the Fageols to form the Fageol Motor Company of Ohio in 1920. Based in Cleveland, the company handled sales in the eastern part of the country. In 1924, the J. G. Brill Company, a Pennsylvania-based trolley car builder, purchased $100,000 worth of stock in Fageol of Ohio, as well as a large stake in the Hall-Scott engine company, but the expansion was short

The earliest Peterbilt models closely resembled their Fageol predecessors, most notably, the egg-crate-style grille.

This 1945 Peterbilt McDonald is thought to be one of a kind, according to its owner Ed Rocha of Rocha Valley Enterprises. The unique truck was built to haul goods from the railyards. Model number 14L is stamped on the frame.

lived. In 1925, J. G. Brill merged with the American Car and Foundry Company and transferred its stock in Fageol Motor Company of Ohio and Hall-Scott to a new corporate entity, the American Car and Foundry Motors Company. William and Frank Fageol kept their Oakland company, and in 1927 they started the Twin Coach Company in Kent, Ohio, to produce a new type of bus they called the "Twin Coach." Through both companies, the Fageol brothers were considered to be instrumental pioneers in public transportation.

The California company continued to build trucks, and through the 1920s and 1930s, Fageol built trucks that featured a distinctive look. The design called for a row of louvered vents on top of the engine hood. According to Wes Hammond in the Lincoln Highway Association's fall 2001 newsletter, *The Traveler*, Fageol offered three basic truck models from its Oakland factory: the Cub, the Bear, and the Flyer. The Cub was rated at 1 1/2 tons, the Bear was 2 tons, and the Flyer was rated at 3 tons. In their last years, an aluminum grille was added to the front of the radiator and the cabs were made with rounded corners. The trucks retained their louvered hood vents.

Despite producing a seemingly popular product, Fageol was unable to survive the turmoil caused by the Great Depression and entered bankruptcy in 1932. The company continued operating during bankruptcy under the control of its creditors as Fageol Truck and Coach. The company was on the brink of closing down in 1938 but was sold to a visionary businessman who had built his business in the timberlands of the American Northwest.

Like many other great products, Peterbilt trucks sprang from a need. T. A. Peterman, a logger and wood products producer located in Tacoma, Washington, had been rebuilding surplus military vehicles to pull logs out of the forest for his logging operation. He had also reportedly owned some Fageol trucks and was familiar with their design. When he found out that the Fageol truck building company was available for sale in 1939, he bought it, and the company joined his other businesses under the Peterman Manufacturing banner. Peterman planned to redesign the Fageol logging truck for his operations, and the Peterbilt nameplate was born. According to numerous historical accounts, the name "Peterbilt" was used on wood products produced by one of his companies and was also applied to the new trucks.

According to the company's history, Peterman built 14 trucks in the first year and 82 in 1940. During World War II, commercial truck building slowed, but the company did build some trucks under government contract. The first models were based on Fageol designs, but soon the company was putting its own stamp on the design and manufacture of its trucks. Peterman had first-hand experience with logging and other trucks and was said to have sent his engineers out to work sites to see for themselves the various conditions under which trucks had to operate.

Peterman died in 1945 and two years later his widow sold the company, but not the land, to a group of company managers. The company, which had operated as part of the Peterman Manufacturing Company, was renamed Peterbilt Motors Company. The company continued to grow under the ownership group until 1958, when Mrs. Peterman decided to sell the property on which the Peterbilt plant was located. Once again, it looked like this might be the end of the truck company, but the Washington-based Pacific Car and Foundry, later renamed PACCAR, bought Peterbilt Motors and it became a division of Pacific Car in 1960. Pacific Car also owned the Kenworth Truck Company.

The impact of the new ownership was immediate. Pacific Car built a new plant for Peterbilt in Newark, California. Production soared the following year and grew to more than 1,000 trucks by the early 1960s. The focus on quality and durability continued throughout the company's growth. As demand for trucks increased, another plant was added in Nashville, Tennessee, in 1969. Manufacturing operations at the California plant were eventually moved to a new facility in Denton, Texas, in 1980, and the corporate headquarters was moved there in the early 1990s.

Like many truck makers, Peterbilt built its trucks according to how a customer planned to use them. The same model truck could be specified with a range of components to fit a variety of applications. Although the trucks within a model range shared similar components and cabs, each truck was essentially a custom-made vehicle built for a customer's planned

The interior of Ed Rocha's 1945 Peterbilt 14L is as close to original condition as possible.

This restored 1945 Peterbilt features a slotted bumper with tapered ends. Note the Peterbilt badge is painted to match the truck's color. The original truck probably had side badges above the air vents.

This is what John Teresi's 1948 Model 270 DD looked like before it was restored in the early 1970s. It had belonged to Battaglia Trucking, a nearby trucking outfit owned by Teresi's cousin.

application. Certain components for highway-use trucks were constructed with alloy metals to reduce weight. Peterbilt was one of the first commercial truck manufacturers to use aluminum for weight reduction. Vocational trucks, those built for off-road work such as logging, were constructed with heavier, stronger metals, double frames, and other measures to increase durability under harsh conditions.

Antique truck collectors tend to classify earlier Peterbilts in three categories: those built from the time Peterman took over until the end of World War II, those models introduced and built from just after the war until 1949, and the trucks produced in the 1950s. Examples of these early classics can be found throughout the country, but especially in California and other West Coast states. Petes

in the early years were sold primarily in California, Oregon, and Washington, and that is where most of the old-timers were put out to pasture, discovered by a collector, and ultimately restored.

In the early years of the company, Peterbilt designers began to develop the styling touches that ultimately became recognizable throughout the world. They also established a tradition of craftsmanship and manufacturing quality for which Peterbilt trucks are known.

Peterbilt made 14 trucks in the first year of production at the Oakland manufacturing facility, according to Henry Rasmussen's *Peterbilt: The Class of the Industry*. Among these were Model 334s and 260s. These models featured the Fageol egg-crate-style grille cover and curved, rounded bumpers. Early sales literature

Teresi Trucking upgraded the dash to accommodate modern instruments when this 1948 truck was restored in the early 1970s. Other touches include the diamond-pattern headliner and doors.

touts Peterbilt's all-steel, welded cab construction. The cab top, doors, and back were made separately to exact specifications so a damaged door or other cab part could be easily replaced without having to replace the whole cab. The cabs were lined with fitted plywood to insulate against road and engine noise. Leather bucket seats or a straight bench seat could be specified. Driver comfort and ease of operation were key considerations for Peterbilt designers.

Peterbilt eventually moved the headlights from bumper mounts, as shown on this restored 1945 Model 270, to pod mounts on the radiator shell, where they remain on today's traditional models.

Power options included diesel, gasoline, and butane engines from Waukesha, Cummins, and Hall-Scott. Cummins provided diesel engines, while Waukesha and Hall-Scott specialized in gasoline powerplants. The first letter of a two-letter suffix that followed the model numbers of these early trucks was either a G, indicating gasoline power, or a D, which signified a diesel engine. Because of the diesel engines' durability and better fuel economy, gasoline engines eventually ceased being an option for most heavy commercial truck applications.

The Model 260 was a chain-drive single-drive-axle truck. The base gasoline-powered unit has a gross vehicle weight of 32,000 pounds, which made it a Class 7 truck by current standards. Diesel-powered 260s had a gross vehicle weight of 37,000 pounds.

The Model 334 was a dual drive and also featured the same engine choices, but the heavier truck had gross vehicle weights up to 44,000 pounds. The Model 344 was a heavier truck that weighed in at 13,750 pounds for just the cab and chassis, some 1,000 pounds more than the Model 334.

While you can't really see it in the trucks built during the company's first period, those introduced after the end of World War II and in the 1950s carried the first hints of that distinctive Peterbilt style: a long, high hood with a tall grille. These designs moved away from the rounded grilles and curved bumpers of the early Fageol-based models and began to look like Peterbilts. The first models to do away with the Fageol egg-crate grille were Models 270, 344, and 354. In the early Peterbilts, a model number beginning with a 2 represented a single-drive or tax-axle truck, while a model number beginning with a 3 was a dual-drive, three-axle truck.

The 270 was a single-drive truck produced from 1941 to 1949. The first models featured a 6-inch steel-channel bumper with a hardwood insert. The standard Waukesha six-cylinder engine supplied 127 horsepower. On the heavy-duty version, a Cummins HB 600 provided 150 horsepower. More than 300 Model 270s were built.

Great examples of Peterbilt's classic butterfly hood and the second-generation nameplate can be found on this restored 1948 270.

The Model 344 was a dual drive, while the 354 featured a heavy-duty dual drive and stiffer suspension. These two models were updated as the Model 345 and 355 in 1945. The dual-drive, heavy-duty Model 345 proved to be the company's most popular truck in those days, with almost 500 trucks built of that particular model.

By the late 1940s, these models came with a distinctive bumper, the top of which was in front of the bottom of the radiator. To improve airflow to the radiator, the bumper had four horizontal slots in the front with tow hooks attached to the top of the bumper.

Chapter 2

PETERBILTS AND THE BIRTH OF LONG-HAUL TRUCKING

The post–World War II years saw the beginning of a long period of economic expansion in the United States. It was a boom time. Industries grew, cities and towns expanded, and farms prospered. The population began to spread out with new subdivisions springing up in all parts of the country. The trucking industry was a full participant. As new homes, stores, and businesses were being built, trucks were carrying the lumber, concrete, and other building materials needed for the expansions.

Page 26: This 1963 Peterbilt Model 351 with a sleeper box, owned by Gary Robey, shows the horizontal radiator shutters and long butterfly-style hood of the classic model. Trucks such as the Model 351 were used in a number of trucking applications and were among the vanguard of the long-haul legends that would follow.

Peterbilt was growing during this time, as well. The company built just over 2,050 trucks from 1939 to 1949, but truck production really began to pick up at the close of World War II. After building trucks for military use during the war, Peterbilt engineers put some of the lessons learned from their work to use in designing the next generation of trucks. During this time, Peterbilt continued to lead the way with its line of sturdy trucks. Its dump trucks, loggers, and cement mixers were routinely on the job throughout the West. As the company developed a more extensive dealership network, truckers in the East began buying Peterbilts.

Peterbilt introduced 20 models between 1949 and 1959. The company's production more than doubled with more than 4,000 trucks built between 1950 and 1959. It was during this time that the company began developing models that, with occasional updates through the years, would dominate in their market niches for two decades or more. This was the mode of operation the company followed through the years. A number of Peterbilt classics hit the road during this time, such as the Model 351 and Model 281 introduced in 1954. Both of these trucks were produced up until the 1970s and demonstrated the timeless quality of Peterbilt's design.

Underlying the booming truck market and expanding economy were new roads. Public officials have long understood the link between transportation and economic growth. Road building has always been an important government function, according to an article marking the 50th anniversary of the Interstate Highway System by the Federal Highway Department's Richard

Weingroff. In 1806, President Thomas Jefferson signed a bill that authorized the building of the Cumberland Highway, a national road from the East Coast to the Ohio River. Roads, canals, and railways connected communities and facilitated commerce.

Early federal highway plans focused on inter-city routes that would tie major urban areas together. Trucks carried the bulk of the freight moving within and between cities, but long-haul freight primarily moved by rail up until the end of World War II. While federal highway officials were funding new U.S. highways between cities in the 1930s, there was little thought of increasing the role of trucks in long-haul freight movements. In fact, trucking's share of moving domestic freight during the war dropped to only 5.6 percent of total ton-miles in 1943. By the 1950s, however, trucking's share had climbed to 17 percent of total freight ton-miles. Trucking companies were already running trips of 700 miles or more, from the Southeast to the Northeast and through the Midwest. The trucking industry's share of freight continued to grow. The U.S. Department of Transportation's Bureau of Transportation Statistics reported that by 2005, trucks accounted for 28 percent of domestic freight ton-miles. If based on tons alone, trucks carry almost 70 percent of the nation's freight, reports the American Trucking Association (ATA).

In many areas, trucks are the only freight option available to keep store shelves stocked and fuel station tanks full. Trucks continue to travel more miles each year. Class 8 trucks accounted for 130.5 billion miles, or 32 percent of the 414 billion miles all weight classes drove for business purposes in 2005, as reported by the ATA. The trucking industry is a vital link between businesses and their customers. Whether it's hauling lumber and other raw materials out of a forest, delivering materials to manufacturing facilities, hauling finished goods from the factory to the store, or transporting building materials to job sites, trucks have become indispensable to our economy. This is reiterated by one of ATA's slogans: "Good Stuff—Trucks Bring It." Indeed, trucks have become so important in keeping America's stores stocked that a disruption of truck service for only a few days can leave store shelves empty.

Key to the growing role of trucks in long-haul freight transportation was the interstate system. President Dwight D. Eisenhower signed the Federal Aid Highway Act in 1956, which specifically formed a funding mechanism for building the interstate freeway system. While the Federal Highway Act of 1944 designated a national system of interstate highways, it did not create a program to fund such highways. The 1956

continued on page 34

This beautifully restored 1949 Peterbilt 350, owned by Jerry Howard, shows the trademark vertical radiator shutters. This picture was taken at the 2007 Stars & Stripes Paul K. Young Memorial Truck Beauty Show in Louisville, Kentucky. It's safe to say very few trucks of that time had the custom aftermarket sleeper compartment Howard has added to his truck, but the classic narrow-nose profile is unmistakable.

This beautifully restored and modified 1957 Peterbilt 350 illustrates
the level of customization Peterbilt owners bring to their rides. The
truck, owned by A&L Truck Supply of Fresno, California, was displayed
by Juan Gonzalez at the 2007 TruckerFest held at the Alamo Petro in
Sparks, Nevada.

This restored 1954 Model 280 was converted into a motor home by a partner in Courtland TruckWorks, a truck shop in Courtland, California, that specializes in restoring old Petes.

This photo from the early 1960s shows two of John Teresi's children and a new Model 351 needle-nose. This truck features a straight steel bumper, which indicated it was probably built in the early to mid-part of the model's production run from 1954 to 1976.

This is a 1954 Peterbilt operated by Teresi Trucking. This truck was probably a Model 350.

This restored and modified 1954 was spotted at a truck beauty show held in celebration of the Muralt's Travel Plaza in Missoula, Montana, during August 2000.

continued from page 29

bill rectified the situation. The first project funded under the new act was an 8-mile stretch of interstate in Missouri that eventually became part of I-70. The act called for 41,000 miles of interstate highway. Almost 47,000 miles have been built in the last 50 years. As noted in the previous chapter, President Eisenhower had first-hand experience of transcontinental truck travel from a 1919 army truck train. His experiences reinforced his notion that good roads were not only necessary for national defense purposes, but were necessary for continued economic growth.

Traveling the interstate highways over the last 50 years is where Peterbilt made its reputation as a long-haul legend. The trucks' proven durability, driver comfort, and quality engineering made Peterbilt the truck that truckers wanted to own and to drive. In

1949, the company was poised to meet the challenges and demands of a growing economy and introduced nine new models, expanding its truck line to include cab-over models, as well as conventional trucks. Among the models Peterbilt introduced after World War II were the 350 and 280. They were long-nose classic-style conventionals with a tall, thin radiator profile that proved to be popular trucks for a variety of applications. Models 380, 360, 390, 370, and the 360 cab-over were also introduced that year. The 350 was by far the most popular of these models, followed by the 280.

Peterbilt made about 850 Model 350s and almost 400 Model 280s between 1949 and 1957. The longest production run of the other models introduced in 1949 was for the 360, which was built until 1956. The radiator for these models featured vertical shutters, which were different from the horizontal shutters found on the Model 270.

The Model 350, Peterbilt's most popular truck during this period, featured the company's trademark fully enclosed, welded-steel cab. The dual-drive-axle truck was available in four wheelbases from 193 1/4 to 240 inches. The bumper for the Model 350 and other trucks built during this time no longer had four slots in the front and tow hooks on the top. With the radiator sitting more above the bumper, the bumper did not need the slots for airflow. Instead of attaching tow hooks on the top of the bumper, the hooks on these trucks were attached to the frame and accessed via two square holes in the bumper called "tow eyes." The bumper was tapered at the ends. With the bumper lower on these models, the headlights were moved higher and attached to either side of the radiator cowl.

The Model 280 was a single-drive truck with wheelbases from 175 to 227 inches. It was similar in many ways to the Model 350 and was the company's second most popular model when it was introduced. Both of these trucks were also available as cab-over models. The dual-drive Model 360 was a longer-wheelbase version of the Model 350, with wheelbases offered from 198 5/8 to 240 inches. The 360 was built for heavy-duty work and featured a full double-channel frame for heavy-duty operations.

Unlike the Model 350, the Model 370 did not have skirted fenders. The 370 was built for heavy-duty work, such as logging, and featured a steel bar attached to the bumper to protect the radiator. Like other Peterbilt logging trucks, this model also had a

wooden platform on the roof where a worker could stand during loading and unloading operations, which gave it a distinct look. The Model 370 was available in wheelbases from 198 5/8 to 240 inches. The Model 380 looked similar to the 370, but with a wheelbase that was about 4 inches shorter on the base model. The Model 380 was built until 1954. The Model 390, built from 1949 until 1953, was another logging truck similar to the 370 and 380, but with a 197 1/4-inch wheelbase on the base model.

Even though seven new models rolled out in 1949, Peterbilt was not content to rest on its laurels and

continued on page 42

This 1952, restored by Lucky Fruit & Produce, was on display at a truck show hosted by Tenco Truck Service of Sacramento in 1988.

The Red Oval is Not Always Red or Oval

Peterbilt began using the red oval name badge with a deep red background, chrome lettering, and chrome border in the early 1950s. That oval badge has become as much a part of the Peterbilt legacy as the trucks and can be found on all types of Peterbilt merchandise including hats, jackets, shirts, backpacks, golf balls, and many other goods.

Histories of the company say the oval was the third name badge adopted by the company. Apparently, the third time was the charm, as that symbol has become as recognizable as the Mercedes-Benz star is to automobile aficionados. The very first Peterbilts had the name in its familiar script running along the side of the truck's hood. A rectangular badge was then used for a few years until the red oval made its mark on the truck and on trucking history.

The second-generation Peterbilt badge featured the name in a rectangular plate, as on this restored 1945 vintage truck.

For some Pete owners, customizing their truck is an ongoing and seemingly never-ending process, and the name badge is no exception. Truckers have found numerous ways to modify or customize this symbol of class. Whether it's painting the oval to match the truck's overall paint scheme or other changes, Peterbilt owners are known to express their individuality and pride in their ride.

On these pages, we'll take a look at an "old-style" Peterbilt badge and a number of red ovals that aren't red, but all Peterbilt nonetheless.

Kris Gaare's 1998 Peterbilt 379 sports a black oval emblazoned with the truck's nickname.

The 2007 379 uses an old-style rectangular logo with chrome letters on a background color that matches the truck's paint.

Matching the truck's paint scheme is a popular way to customize the Peterbilt oval, such as this blue one.

Truckers sometimes use the oval and other elements of the truck's front end as contrast points for the truck's paint scheme.

Some truckers pass on painting the background of a traditional oval and replace it with something else, such as this nameplate.

The oval is unchanged on this truck, but there is a little extra customization to express the owner's individuality.

Most of the time, the background matches the truck's paint, but in this instance the script matches the truck and the background is a different color. Note the extra design elements that further distinguish this look.

Another background color is used to match the truck. In this case the color is orange.

This Limited Edition 379 sports a black background in the oval to match the truck's color scheme.

The old-style nameplate makes an appearance on this Model 379's hood to reinforce the truck's nickname as *Tired Iron*.

This old badge was spotted on a 1997 Model 379. The badge and a few other touches, including old-style headlights, gave the truck a vintage feel, even though in Peterbilt terms it's relatively new.

Ringsby Truck Lines Inc. of Denver, Colorado, was one of the bigger western carriers. Ringsby had Peterbilt bubble noses like this Model 350; however, this one looks like it was an owner-operator leased on with Ringsby for a trip lease with Long Transportation Co. of Detroit, Michigan. The rig was in Ringsby's reefer division and pulled a Dorsey reefer trailer. The Model 350 was produced from 1950 to 1959. Total production was 299. *Neil Sherff*

continued from page 35

introduced three more models in 1954 that would carry the Pete nameplate for the next two decades. These trucks were the first of many Peterbilt models over the years that enjoyed production runs of 20 years or more. A brand-new truck bought in 1970 might sit right next to the same model built in 1955.

One of the classics introduced in 1954 was Peterbilt's venerable Model 351, which remained in production until 1976. More than 7,000 Model 351s were built during the model's 22-year production run, which made it the company's most popular model at that time. It was versatile, durable, and good looking. Sales of the truck dropped when Peterbilt introduced the Model 359 in

The Model 281 was the single axle in the conventional line. The one seen here was used to pull the Dorsey moving van trailer for Republic Van & Storage Co. A sort of small sleeper box was added for cross-country runs. Notice all the permit listings on the sleeper box door. This was also part of the dress code of the time. *Ron Adams Collection*

Here we see another Peterbilt Model 350, but this time as a conventional type truck. These truck-trailer combinations were very popular in the western states. This model was known as the "iron nose" Pete. Notice that the fenders on both the conventional and the cab-over engine have a side skirt. The company is undentifed. The 350 conventional was produced from 1949 to 1957, with a total of 847 units manufactured. *Ron Adams Collection*

The Model 281 refers to the tractor as a single axle. The one shown here is owned by Max Binswanger Trucking Inc., of Santa Fe Springs, California. Its job is to pull this set of Butler pneumatic tanker trailers. By the mid-1960s, the 281 and 351 both had tilt hoods. Max Binswanger always had his equipment looking sharp. *Ron Adams Collection*

1967. The 351 was updated throughout its run with new interiors, chrome options, and a wider range of engines.

The 351 and the single-drive 281 were the first Peterbilt highway trucks to feature fenders without skirts. They were also among the first Petes to sport the narrow, long-nose profile with horizontal radiator shutters. Like their predecessors, these models were versatile and used in a variety of applications from general freight hauling to local and regional delivery, bulk, and tank hauling. Over its 20-year run, the Model 351 established a reputation for performance, classic looks, and top quality. These trucks racked up millions of miles in all kinds of applications and provided one of the most popular long-haul rides. Some are still working, while others can often be found at truck beauty shows or other venues where historical truck enthusiasts gather.

Early versions of the Model 351 were equipped with a straight, steel bumper, similar to previous Pete models. Later models received a bumper that was tapered on the ends in a gull-wing style. Later models could be specified with a polished-aluminum grille surround and other custom features.

From the grove to the packing house is where this load of oranges was heading. Hauling the load for Sunkist Growers is a Peterbilt Model 281 pulling a set of Fruehauf agricultural trailers. Double trailers were also a common sight on the western highways. The tractor had a 64-inch cab. Sleeper cabs were not necessary on trips like these. The 281 was produced from 1956 to 1959 with 123 units manufactured. *Ron Adams Collection*

The basic model had a bumper-to-back-of-cab (BBC) span of 119 1/4 inches, as opposed to the 130-inch BBC of the Models 350 and 280. The A and M models had a welded, all-aluminum cab that was fully insulated with 1 1/2-inch fiberglass and finished with an embossed aluminum cab liner. The heavy-duty version, the ST model, had an all-steel cab. West Coast–style mirrors were standard equipment. The base model had a gross volume weight of 49,000 pounds and a gross combined volume weight of 76,800 pounds, making the Model 351 a workhorse in every sense of the word. A 250-horsepower Cummins that generated 685 lb-ft of torque was standard.

Like a lot of other Petes, Models 351 and 281 had either major or small parts in numerous movies and television shows. A Model 281 with a tag axle played a major role in the 1971 movie *Duel*, in which a motorist is terrorized by a trucker driving a dirty, menacing truck. The driver's face is never shown in the movie, so the truck takes on the leading role of villain in the movie. A Model 351 appears in the original *Texas Chainsaw Massacre*, and in the 2003 remake of the horror film. The Internet Movie Cars Database, www.imcdb.org, lists 10 web pages of movies and television shows in which a Peterbilt can be seen or plays a major role, including *Convoy*; *Smokey and the Bandit*; *Breaker*; *The A-Team*; and *Desperate Housewives*, just to name a few.

A tilt-hood version of the 351, the Model 358, began production in 1965 and was produced through 1976. The truck featured an air-assist hood-tilting mechanism to open the aluminum hood, as opposed to the butterfly hood of the Model 351. Drivers could check and fill fluid levels via outside access without opening the hood. The Model 351 is popular with collectors and truck hobbyists, and restored versions can fetch upwards of $25,000.

The Model 381, a heavy-duty off-road truck also introduced in 1954, was in production for 20 years. The sales of the Model 381 never approached those of the 351 or 281, but the truck found great acceptance in construction, mining, aggregate, and dump truck applications. It was built of all steel, including the cab, and included double- or triple-construction frames.

The Model 381's fenders were walk-in fenders that were wide, square-shaped, and flat on the top. A walkway that ran from the rear of the fender to the rear of the cab provided additional walk space for workers during loading operations.

The Model 381 was available in 182 3/4-inch, 188 1/8-inch, and 201 5/8-inch wheelbases. It was a long-nosed truck with a BBC measurement of more than 135 inches.

This Model 351 was owned by a man whose last name was Guerrieipi. He leased his rig to Love & Sons Potato Co. in Denver, Colorado. Production on this model started in 1954 and went up to 1976. Some styling changes were made through the 22-year run. A narrow bumper was one of the changes, as was the butterfly hood. The cab roof was also separate. Around 1960, the roof and cab were one piece. The trailer is a utility that looks like it could be an ex-Interstate Motor Lines trailer. *Neil Sherff*

Chapter 3

THE 1960S, 1970S, AND PETERBILT'S FIRST LEGEND: THE MODEL 359

In the late 1960s and early 1970s, long-haul trucking began to establish itself not only as a means to move goods, but also as a cultural touchstone. As the interstate highway system grew, so did the number of truckers running long-haul. Bigger, more powerful engines became available and truck design reflected these changes. As trucks began making longer runs, sleeper boxes became more popular and truck makers focused on more comfortable interior environments. Longer runs also meant

Page 46: Johnny Hidalgo of Sandvik Trucking in Valley Center, California, won a trophy at a 2007 truck show in Las Vegas with this 1987 Model 359. Sandvik runs all Peterbilts and owner Bill Sandvik has won numerous best-of-show awards for his customized Petes.

that reliability, which is always a factor for truck buyers, was now the long-haul customer's primary concern. As the miles racked up, truckers wanted to be confident their trucks would not break down along a lonely stretch of highway. Trucks had to meet these new expectations, and the Peterbilts of this era did just that.

Running long-haul was a different kind of trucking. Truckers were on the road for weeks at a time. Trucks and truckers were featured in songs such as "Haulin' Freight," "Six Days On the Road," "Phantom 309," and "Truck Driving Man" that populated the airwaves. Truck stops began popping up along the new interstates to sell fuel to these long-haul truckers and earned their own place in popular culture via songs, movies, and television shows. Diners catering to truckers soon followed and the quality of an establishment's food was often measured by the number of trucks parked out front. The 1970s saw a rash of trucker-themed movies from 1971's *Duel*, directed by Steven Spielberg and starring Dennis Weaver and a Peterbilt 281, to the first *Smokey and the Bandit* movie, which came out in 1977. Perhaps because of the songs or the movies, just about everybody at that time wanted a CB radio in their automobile.

Whether they are a company driver or an owner-operator, truck drivers are on their own most work days. This pertains more so to long-haul drivers than local drivers who return to the home terminal at the end of each shift. Of course, fleet managers tell drivers where and when to pick up the next load, but there is little to no direct supervision while a driver is on the road. What supervision there may have been was long

distance. Trucking fleets must trust their drivers to do the job correctly, efficiently, and safely—there is no other choice. For driver-owners, the work relationship they had with truck fleets was different than that of a company driver, but the job responsibilities were the same and there was the added responsibility of owning the truck.

The truck was the driver-owner's business, home, and most important tool all rolled into one. That's why driving truck became more than a job for many in the industry. Driving truck was a lifestyle. The type of truck one drove said a lot about who was driving it. Your truck offered clues to the kind of business professional you were, the kind of service you offered,

This 1965 Model 351 was restored by Courtland TruckWorks and is an example of the "needle nose" Pete, says TruckWorks owner Darrow Thomson, Jr. At one time, the truck was driven by Thomson's dad. "Back then, when we got in new trucks, people would ask my dad why he wanted to drive that old truck. Now of course, people love these old things," Thomson said.

This 1973 Model 288, owned by Bob Thrift of Umailta, Florida, was proudly displayed at the 2007 75 Chrome Shop Truck Beauty Show held in Wildwood, Florida.

and the kind of person you were. Arriving to pick up or drop off a load in a dirty, broken-down piece of junk said your business was barely getting by. Such a truck said you were probably not reliable and that it was dumb luck that the load was delivered on time. Trucking companies and driver-owners who were serious about their business wanted to deliver a different message. They wanted their trucks to affirm their commitment to their business, customers, and employers. They wanted their trucks to say, "We will do a good job; you can count on it." The trucks most preferred by many of these long-haul truckers, especially owner-operators, were Peterbilts because the trucks did not just assert dependable and reliable truck service, they screamed "class." As one long-time industry veteran noted, "For a Peterbilt owner, it's more than a truck. You can tell by how they take care of their trucks."

Peterbilt had already established itself as the premium truck brand by 1960. The late Ted Engs, who was president of one of the oldest Peterbilt dealerships in California until it was sold in the 1990s, recalled in an interview published in the October 1990 issue of the California Dump Truck Association's magazine, that his father had originally sold Diamond T trucks when he first got into the truck business. The elder Engs jumped at a chance to operate a Peterbilt dealership because they felt Peterbilt produced the superior product. The company was planning to produce many more. Under the ownership of the Pacific Car and Foundry, the company opened a new factory in Newark, California, in 1960 and built more than 800 trucks there during the first year. By 1969, more than 4,000 Peterbilts were built to meet an increasing demand

for commercial trucks. That demand continued to increase and Peterbilt began producing trucks at its Nashville facility in 1970 and built 684 trucks in the first year.

Also in 1970, the U.S. Congress passed the Clean Air Act, which mandated air pollution standards from various sources, such as factory emissions or motor vehicle emissions. Meeting these requirements, which have been considerably tightened since 1970,

This 1967 Model 358 dump owned by Phil's Trucking of Gardnerville, Nevada, is an example of one of Peterbilt's first tilt-hood models. This shot was taken at the 2003 TruckerFest in Sparks, Nevada.

The Model 359 was one of Peterbilt's most popular models. Today's models in Peterbilt's traditional lineup are direct descendants of the Model 359. This 1986, owned by Dave Smith of Pottsville, Pennsylvania, was participating in a truck show at the 2007 Mid-America Trucking Show in Louisville, Kentucky.

demanded changes in engine and exhaust technologies. That, in turn, meant more engineering challenges for truck makers and manufacturers.

Peterbilt continued to roll out a number of new models throughout the 1960s and 1970s, and each incorporated the latest technological advances in truck manufacturing. It was also during this time that Peterbilt cemented its reputation as first in the class of the long road when it introduced the iconic Model 359 in 1967. It was the company's first wide-nosed

conventional truck. For the next 20 years, the Model 359 was Peterbilt's flagship and set a new standard for quality and performance. It was continually identified as the most preferred conventional in numerous surveys and was updated throughout its production run to incorporate new technologies and comfort features. This truck, perhaps more than any other, said "Peterbilt." Even a dirty or unkempt Model 359 looked impressive, and no other truck at the time dressed up the way a 359 could. When polished and outfitted with an appropriate amount of chrome and lights, absolutely nothing in the commercial trucking universe compares.

Peterbilt was building other great models during this time. Not all of them were over-the-road long-haulers, but several made quite a mark in their respective market niches. One of these was the Model 341, which was made for dump and mixer applications. First built in 1962, the 341 was an instant hit with construction-related trucking companies. Its introduction coincided with a huge building boom that was going on in the 1960s. In the 1990 article mentioned earlier, Ted Engs said that during the early 1960s, it seemed like all the trucks they sold were single-axle tractors that would pull a double-bottom dumper. That changed with the introduction of the 341, according to Engs, because they were able to penetrate a huge percentage of the ready-mix concrete business in his area.

The Model 341 was built for the job. It featured a 113 1/4-inch BBC. For front-end power take-off mixers, the front bumper was extended 17 inches and dropped some. It boasted a 56,000-pound gross volume weight, an all-aluminum cab, aluminum fenders, flywheel or front-engine power take-off, and a 195-horsepower Detroit Diesel engine as standard power. For dump applications, the Model 341 was equipped with a 38,000-pound rear suspension, as opposed to the 34,000-pound setup for mixer work.

Introduced in 1964, the Model 383 was an updated off-highway truck designed for the toughest applications. With a BBC of almost 140 inches, the 383 was an impressive truck with a gross volume weight of 83,000 pounds and a gross combined volume weight of 150,000 pounds, which is enough truck for the hardiest of applications. The frame was made with heat-treated alloy steel with all the parts bolted together for extra strength. The cab was of all-steel construction and the fenders were the flat, walk-on type, also made of steel.

The standard engine for the Model 383 was a Cummins NHC-250 that produced 250 horsepower and 685 lb-ft of torque. The 65,000-pound Rockwell rear axle and 18,000-pound Rockwell front axles were also standard equipment. Unlike the earlier Model 381, the 383 did not have a platform on the cab roof, nor did it have a side platform running on the side of the cab underneath the doors.

The Stabilaire suspension was introduced in 1964 and promised a smoother ride from a lighter-weight yet more durable suspension. The heart of the suspension was a combination of heavy-duty springs and air-load cushions. Leveling valves on either side of the suspension automatically controlled the height of the chassis by regulating the air pressure in the load cushions. Loaded or empty, the suspension was designed to deliver an excellent ride and great

This 1970s vintage Model 359, owned by Wayne Smith of Chalfont, Pennsylvania, competed in the 2007 Paul K. Young Memorial Truck Beauty Show at the Mid-America Trucking Show.

handling ability. Peterbilt said its new suspension would extend the vehicle's life by limiting axle rebound and distributing the load over a wider area to eliminate stress on the truck's frame.

In 1965, Peterbilt began building the Model 358, a tilt-hood version of the venerable 351. It was a precursor to the Model 359. The 358 was produced until 1976 with more than 2,700 trucks built. The Model 288 was a single-drive version. These were Peterbilt's first narrow-nosed tilt hood trucks. The butterfly hood was gone, at least for over-the-road truck models. The hood was a multipiece, all-metal component with an air-assisted tilt mechanism. There were outside checkpoints for oil and coolant levels. For owners of Model 351s and 281s, Peterbilt offered a kit that would convert the hood to a tilt type. The Model 358 featured a polished

Peterbilt trucks lend themselves to customization, as demonstrated by this 1986 Model 359 owned by Jeremy Hassevort of Hamilton, Michigan.

This beautiful and customized 1986 Model 359 competed at the 2007 Stars & Stripes Truck Show event in Wildwood, Florida.

Pages 56–61: Peterbilt offered the Classic 359 in the last year of the popular model's production in 1987. This limited-run batch of trucks featured special insignias and a number of other special features to commemorate the truck's 20-year production run.

aluminum grille surround and had a gross combined volume weight of 76,800 pounds. The Model 358 was built from 1965 to 1976 and proved to be a fairly popular model. More than 2,700 Model 358s and 685 Model 288s were built during their production runs.

The Model 359 went into production in 1967 and became an instant classic, with more than 14,000 units sold between 1967 and 1987. The single-drive Model 289 also started production that year. These first models, with a much wider nose, had a similar two-bar grille with the same horizontal Cadillac split-vane shutter radiator design as the Model 351. This radiator design proved troublesome and was replaced with a three-bar grille radiator that featured shutterless cooling. The truck also featured a polished outer radiator shell and a stainless-steel grille.

Comparing sales materials for an early Model 351 and a Model 359 clearly shows the advances in performance and driver comfort Peterbilts are known for. The 351 cab was described as "hand-welded, all-aluminum construction; fully insulated with 1 1/2 inches of fiberglass." The 351's cab also included an embossed aluminum cab liner, insulated floormats, dual interior sun visors, cigarette lighter and ashtray, and a left-hand armrest. Seating was a Peterbilt-Bostrum Thinline for the driver and the passenger seat was a toolbox with upholstered cushion. A heater or window defroster was optional.

The Model 359's all-aluminum cab was described as "fully insulated with foam" and featured a right-hand door view window, padded vinyl upholstery panels and headliner, black rubber floor mats, and two coat hooks.

The 359 also included a cigarette lighter and ashtray and came standard with a combination fresh-air heater/air conditioner with integral windshield washer. The driver's seat was a Peterbilt UltraRide air-suspension seat, while the passenger side was a nonsuspension seat that also included a storage compartment.

The Model 359 was, and is still, used in all kinds of applications, but was a popular truck for long-haul owner-operators. It was a classy ride in just about every aspect. The 359 featured an aluminum cab with a 119 1/4-inch BBC measurement. Optional BBCs of 113 1/4 and 127 1/4 inches were available to accommodate the engine offerings. These varying hood lengths led to the short-hood, long-hood distinction among the different models. The tilting hood was first made of all metal but was later available in fiberglass. The truck was offered with a variety of engine options up to 475 horsepower. Standard power was a Cummins Big Cam 4 rated at 300 horsepower. Single, round headlights were offered as standard equipment, but rectangular

dual lights were an option. They quickly caught on as a popular specification among truck buyers.

For the first five years, the Model 359 was built with Peterbilt's Unilite cab, noted for its small windows. A new cab, the 1100 series, was introduced around 1972. A 36-inch crawl-through sleeper box was available, as were 36- and 63-inch walk-through boxes. An automotive-style dash was added to the 359 in 1978.

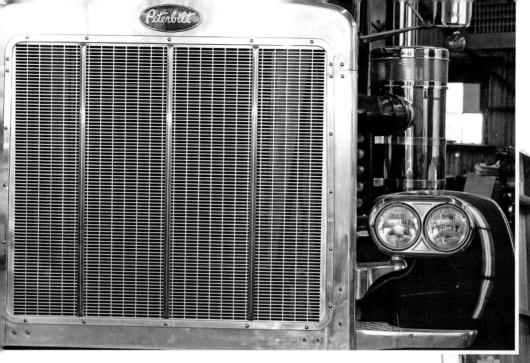

A Model 359 was the first truck to roll off the assembly line at Peterbilt's Denton, Texas, manufacturing facility when the plant began operations in 1980. The company states the plant was focused on building only the 359 when it first opened and had output set at 15 trucks per month. The plant has built about 250,000 various Peterbilt models since then.

The Model 359 was consistently chosen by truckers as the best over-the-road tractor in survey after survey during its run. To mark the passing of this iconic performer, Peterbilt developed a special Model 359 Classic at the end of the truck's production run with a limited output of 359 trucks bearing numbered dash plates and various upgrades. It was a fitting way to say goodbye to a classic truck.

Some Model 359s are still working, while others have been restored and make the truck show rounds. The truck, which established its own legacy during 20 years of production, laid the groundwork for the Model 379—Peterbilt's flagship for the next 20 years.

While the Model 359 was certainly a home run for Peterbilt, the company's engineers never stopped coming up with ways to improve their products or introduce new ones. In 1970, Peterbilt brought out

61

The Model 341 was the dump truck line. The one we see here is known as a transfer dump. This one was owned by the Owl Truck Co. and is getting loaded with the goods for a construction site. The transfer trailer was made by Utility.
Ron Adams Collection

the Model 348 mixer chassis that featured a slightly sloped, fiberglass tilt hood. It was an important feature for mixer applications since they so often operate within confined spaces at job sites. The 348 replaced the Model 341, and a 6x6 version of the Model 348 was also built during this time.

The Model 346 was built from 1974 to 1976 and featured a 109-inch set-back front axle for some mixer and dump applications that required hauling heavy

loads. The 346 had an aluminum butterfly hood with detachable side panels.

The Model 353, introduced in 1972, was a heavy-duty version of the Model 359 and replaced the heavy-duty versions of the Model 351. The Model 353 had a long hood with a BBC dimension of 177 1/4 inches. The hood was an aluminum butterfly type and the fenders were heavy-duty flat-topped steel with a safety walk anti-skid surface. A 350-horsepower Cummins

The Peterbilt conventional took on a somewhat new look in 1967. The new model was the 359 and had the tilt hood with a 1,444-square-inch frontal area. The standard engine was Cummins NHC-350 with other engines as options. The main transmission was a Dana-Spicer four-speed with a three-speed auxiliary. The 359 was made from 1967 to 1987 with over 14,200 units produced. *Harry Patterson*

NTC-350 was the standard power option. The heavy-duty rear suspension had a 55,000-pound capacity.

A tandem-axle Model 353 was also built and featured a severe-service cab with all-steel back panels, roof panels, and windshield mask. The hood of this particular model had steel slide-in sides for engine access and flat steel fenders with the anti-skid surface.

The Model 387 was introduced in 1975 and was produced until 1982. It was another off-road, heavy-duty work truck. It had a heat-treated, 110,000-psi frame, severe-service front cab mount, steel crossties, and steel cross-members under the cab. A 350-horsepower Cummins Big Cam II engine provided the power and Rockwell 65,000-pound rear axles carried the load. The axle ratings were up to 28,000 pounds in the front and 150,000 pounds in the rear. This truck also had flat fenders and a 54 3/4-inch setback axle. The 126-inch hood was a butterfly type with removable side panels.

Here we have a Model 352, but this one is of the conventional type that also had the narrow bumper of the early 1960s. A sleeper box was added, along with dual chrome stacks and a custom paint job of the time to finish it off. No chrome was spared on the breather. The trailer is a Utility reefer. The owner is from Gothenberg, Nebraska. The polished-aluminum wheels make this tractor the pride of the road. *Neil Sherff*

Blazing its way through the trails of the logging country is this Model 359 with a load of timber bound for the lumber mill. Strong and rugged trucks were needed to handle the challenges of log hauling, so this lumber company put the Peterbilt to the test. Of course, it passed the test with honors. *Photo Illustrators*

The Model 359 also grew bigger when Peterbilt introduced their new 60-inch flat-roof sleeper box. They also started offering the Texas-size bumper. A lot of chrome and polished aluminum was standard on the 359, but a lot more options were of chrome. The company in this case is Chuck-Wagon Express. When you look at a tractor like this one, it shows how much pride the Peterbilt owners take in their equipment. *Neil Sherff*

Like other off-highway trucks, it had flat steel fenders with an anti-skid walking surface.

As the 1970s drew to a close, Peterbilt had again raised the bar for truck manufacturing. The company's products were being used in every trucking application imaginable, at least in the heavier weight classes. With the addition of the company's Nashville plant, production zoomed during the period, with more than 90,000 trucks built from 1960 to 1979. Peterbilt's legendary durability meant that many of the trucks were still running hard 20 or more years after their build date.

Chapter 4

ERA OF A
LONG-HAUL LEGEND

The trucking industry changed tremendously in the 1980s. The nation's economy was declining at the beginning of 1980, which was tough on all industries, especially trucking. The industry received a huge economic boost when President Jimmy Carter signed the Motor Carrier Act of 1980 that ended the era of strict trucking regulations by limiting the Interstate Commerce Commission's (ICC) authority over trucking companies.

The federal government had been regulating interstate transportation since the Interstate Commerce Commission was formed in 1887

Page 66: *The traditional style of a Peterbilt 379, coupled with an eye-catching paint scheme, creates a striking image, such as this 1994 owned by James Davis of Medford, Oregon. This picture was taken at the 2007 TruckerFest in Sparks, Nevada.*

to regulate the railroads. When trucking became a viable mode for transporting goods, the railroads lobbied the ICC to regulate trucks, as well. Congress obliged by passing the Motor Carrier Act of 1935, which required truckers to obtain authority from the ICC to operate in interstate trade. The commission also regulated which truckers could run which routes and which truckers could haul which goods. You might have the authority to run one product from St. Louis to New York, but not the authority to haul another type of freight back to St. Louis. Backhauls were difficult to find. Existing truckers were grandfathered into the new system, but entry for new trucking companies was very difficult. Truckers had to file their rates with the

Jerry Beaudoin's 2007 Black Peterbilt 379 with a J&J dump trailer takes the customization trend to a new level. The wide, low bumper (a favorite among Pete owners these days) contains the roll-over headlights. This shot was taken in Louisville, Kentucky, during the spring of 2007.

Grover Shurvington's 1998 extended hood 379 hauls a Polar Fuel Transport trailer in this picture taken in Louisville during the spring of 2007.

government and other truckers, or even railroad and shipping concerns. Truckers were allowed to inspect the rates and file protests against the rates.

In 1948, truckers were exempted from antitrust laws so they could set rates together as "bureaus." This situation created a closed industry and artificially inflated freight rates. In addition, it was in the interest of carriers that held ICC authority to oppose new applications and effectively keep potential competitors out of the business. Writing in the *Concise*

Alex Fimbres of Apple Valley, California, has plenty of lights on his teal green 2005 379. Fimbres' son suggested the Transformers motif for the fifth wheel cover.

Encyclopedia of Economics, economist Thomas Gale Moore said that between 1940 and 1980, "New or expanded authority to transport goods was almost impossible to secure unless no one opposed an application." Even requests for authority to haul over

The last 1,000 Model 379s Peterbilt made were called the Legacy Class Edition and featured custom touches like special logo treatments on the grille, hood, and under the headlights.

routes not being served could be opposed because truckers with existing authority had first dibs on these new routes. The only way a new trucking firm could haul on the interstate was to purchase the rights from someone who already had those rights. Moore said that the authority to haul some types of cargo over certain routes costs "hundreds of thousands of dollars" by the 1970s.

Troy Points' 2003 379 and East Flatbed present a study in black and chrome. Points hails from Salem, Oregon, and was at the TruckerFest in Sparks, Nevada.

The 1980 Motor Carrier Act still required truckers to obtain authority through the ICC, but it eliminated regulations on commodities and routes. It also made it easier for new trucking companies to get interstate authority, and it was easier for them to compete on rates. States were still allowed to regulate rates and entry for truckers doing strictly intrastate hauling, but state regulation was eliminated in 1994 with the Airport Improvement Act, which prohibited states from regulating trucking, except for safety and insurance requirements. Congress abolished the ICC in 1995.

With deregulation, the number of carriers serving the nation grew substantially and doubled in the first 10 years following the 1980 legislation. Rates went down and service increased. Truckers could serve markets that had been underserved under regulation.

New companies blossomed. Even as long-time trucking firms folded in the new, more competitive environment, new truckers were there to take their place. Business savvy, innovation, customer service, and dedication were the hallmarks of the new truckers. The truck of choice for many of these new truckers was the Peterbilt.

Jason Sutterburg of Canby, Oregon, competed in the 2007 TruckerFest in Sparks, Nevada, with this 2003 Model 379 that features contrasting fenders and straight, dual stacks.

Peterbilt made more than 11,000 trucks in 1980 and production has not dropped below the five-digit range since. A number of other new models were rolled out in the early to mid-1980s, including the Model 397 in 1981, which was Peterbilt's largest truck. The 397 was designed for heavy payloads and large engines with plenty of steel and heavy-duty components used in construction. The frame was made of triple channel steel with the rails running from the front bumper to the rear of the truck. There were no extensions to the frame; it supported the entire truck. The radiator and headlines were protected by steel guards and the bumper was all steel. Engines up to 600 horsepower could be specified with rear axle ratings up to 150,000

pounds for a combined vehicle payload of 500,000 pounds. The truck was built with a severe-duty, heavy aluminum cab structure with steel panels and included flat walk-on fenders and step boards that extended to the back of the cab. The 141-inch butterfly hood was made of steel. Because the truck was designed for large, wide loads, the rearview mirrors were mounted on the fender to allow the driver to see around the load.

The Model 362 cab-over was also introduced in 1981. The Model 310, which had begun production in 1977, was replaced by the Model 320 in 1985. Both of these models will be discussed in later chapters.

But the real action was when Peterbilt rolled out five new models that represented the heart of its truck

Kevin Pascavis of Sussex, Wisconsin, draws a crowd with his 2007 lime green and black Peterbilt 379. Note the extra-tall double stacks.

An orange and grey paint scheme adorns this 2007 Model 379, owned by Roger Rodgers of Locust Grove, Florida.

The traditional style of a Peterbilt 379, coupled with an eye-catching paint scheme, creates a striking image, such as this 1994 owned by James Davis of Medford, Oregon. This picture was taken at the 2007 TruckerFest in Sparks, Nevada.

lineup in 1986. The key model was the 379, which was built to replace the 359. The 379 went on to become a long-haul legend in its own right, but the other models introduced that year were key players, as well. Besides Model 359, other Pete models were retired in the mid-1980s, including Models 289, 349, 353, and 348. Taking their place in the lineup were Model 375, designed for short to medium hauls; Model 377; Model

357 vocational truck; and Model 378, a fiberglass-hood version of the Model 379.

The 375 was built for short hauls and featured an aero-dynamic, slightly sloped and rounded fiberglass hood with a 114-inch BBC. A 285-horsepower Caterpillar 3306B was the standard powerplant with a Fuller seven-speed transmission and Eaton 40,000-pound-capacity tandem axle. The headlights were composite halogen

This 1996 Model 379, owned by Sandvik Trucking, has earned a number of truck show awards with its custom paint scheme and chrome accents.

high beams mounted in the fenders along with the turn signals, as opposed to the traditional method of mounting the lights on a stalk on the side of the hood. The cab was made of aluminum and fully insulated and lined with padded vinyl headliners, back panels, and doors.

The Model 375 was in production until 1995. Model 376, a two-axle version of the Model 375, began production in 1988. It also had a 114-inch BBC with fiberglass hood. Standard power on the 376 was a Cummins C Series rated at 250 horsepower.

Bob Cretton of Montague, California, participated in a 2007 truck show at the Petro truck stop in Sparks, Nevada, with his 1996 Model 379 pulling a Western Curtain van trailer.

This 2000 379 sports a customized grille that is a flashback to earlier models and shows some of the curved surfaces found on the grille of Peterbilt's current aerodynamic lineup.

The Model 377 was Peterbilt's first aerodynamic long-haul tractor. Like the Model 375, the 377 had a fiberglass hood, but with a BBC that measured 122 inches, making the hood about 8 inches longer than the 375. A set-back axle version with a 120-inch BBC was also available, but the shorter hood limited the choice of engines. The fiberglass hood included a spring-assist tilting mechanism that could tilt the hood 90 degrees. It also had the headlights and turn signals mounted in the fenders.

The standard engine on the 377 was a Caterpillar 3406B rated at 310 horsepower and 1,150 lb-ft of torque. Optional engines from Cummins or Caterpillar

with up to 444 horsepower were also available. The 377 could be specified with a variety of sleepers. Roof and cab back fairings could also be specified to increase the truck's aerodynamic characteristics.

The Model 357 was the new workhorse in the product line when it was introduced in 1986. The standard model had a slightly sloped fiberglass hood with a 111-inch BBC and fiberglass fenders. Optional BBCs of 119 or 123 inches were also available to accommodate set-back or set-forward axles. The 123-inch BBC model has a butterfly-type steel hood. Standard power was supplied by a 285-horsepower Caterpillar 3306B, and optional engines with up to 444 horsepower were

This Model 379 is operated by Teresi Trucking of Lodi, California. Note the tool rack mounted behind the sleeper box, which is one of the modifications Teresi makes on all its trucks before they enter service.

available from Cummins. Caterpillar offered engines with up to 425 horsepower.

A variety of severe-service options were available, including flat steel fenders, 23,000-pound front axles, and 52,000-pound rear axles. The truck could also be configured as a 6x6 drive vehicle with power supplied to all six wheel positions. Heavy-duty fuel tanks made from aluminum or steel could fit the demands of just about any job.

THE LEGEND

The Peterbilt Model 379 was introduced in 1986 and served as the company's flagship model until the last one rolled off the assembly line in 2007. It was one of the company's most popular models with more than 230,000 built over its 20-year production run. Reflecting the company's tradition of durable work trucks, Peterbilt reports that more than 89 percent of those trucks are still in operation.

The 379 reflects the long-nose look characteristic of the company's product line. Available in a 119-inch BBC and 127-inch BBC extended model, the 379 is one of the last over-the-road trucks built with an aluminum hood. It features huck-bolt construction, rather than rivets, for increased strength and was offered in both truck and tractor configurations. While it established its legend over the road, the 379 was also a popular vocational truck. It is common to find it hauling dump trailers or outfitted with a mixer body.

Over the course of its lifetime, the 379 was upgraded to take advantage of new technological advances, and there were some interior changes and new sleeper bodies

This Model 379, seen at Muralt's Travel Plaza in Missoula, Montana, helps express its owner's patriotic feelings.

offered. Despite these changes, the 379 retained its bold, hard-working lines and durability. The company refers to its styling as "classic long-nose conventional," to reflect the glory days of trucking and embody the most up-to-date performance and comfort levels of modern trucks.

The 379 was capable of taking the widest range of engines of any truck in its class, all the way up to 600 horsepower. As with all the "custom-made" trucks from Peterbilt, the 379 could be specified with a variety of suspension, transmission, and engine combinations to enable it to handle just about any job. Six different frame rails were available for the

optimum strength-to-weight requirements. It could be configured as a truck or tractor, day cab or sleeper cab. Sleepers were from 36 to 70 inches and offered drivers a wide range of interior options.

The ability to customize is one of the more noticeable attributes of the Model 379 and other Peterbilt models. Owners can specify a wide array of engines, interiors, and sleeper configurations. In the aftermarket, they can find plenty of chrome and stainless-steel accessories, such as exhaust stacks, sun visors, bug screens, fenders, and more that can make each 379 unique in its own way and still retain the classic Pete look.

Cliff and Peggy Watkins won a Best of Show award and $2,500 worth of silver bars with their 1998 379 at a special 25th anniversary celebration for Muralt's Travel Plaza in Missoula, Montana, in August 2000.

The company offered an optional customizing package for the 127-inch BBC extended-hood Model 379 that featured a stainless-steel grille with a punched oval patter, polished aluminum grille bars, premium Donaldson air cleaners with the punched oval pattern on the air intake screens, and a stainless-steel sun visor.

The Model 379 featured Peterbilt's patented Unibilt cab sleeper system that incorporates the cab and sleeper into a single unit. This configuration offered optimum interior space and helped soften the ride. Plus, the sleepers could be removed and a back wall kit installed to enable an over-the-road truck to serve a second life as a day cab in a different application. The cabs are constructed of aluminum alloys for extra strength. The hood tilts 90 degrees for easy service and uses a spring-assisted hood hinge for easy opening.

On top of all the great performance and comfort features found in the Model 379 is the great resale value of the truck. It is among the highest in the industry, with many Model 379s passing through three or more owners.

The Model 379X, which was introduced in 2003, sported polished aluminum fenders, Peterbilt oval-pattern grille, polished aluminum centerline hood accent, and brushed aluminum dash and sleeper trim.

A Model 379 is ready to go to work in Sacramento, California. The 379 is one of Peterbilt's most popular models and used in all types of applications from long-haul to construction.

Other special touches for the 379X were polished aluminum grille bars, 7-inch chromed exhaust stacks, and a chromed Texas-style bumper. The interior featured brushed-aluminum dash panels and matching cab and sleeper trim, leather UltraRide seats, chromed shift lever knob, and other touches.

The last 1,000 Model 379s were designated the Model 379 Legacy Class Edition. Among the features of these special trucks were Legacy Class Edition emblems on the grille and both sides of the cab and a custom dash plate inscribed with the vehicle's production number. The Legacy Class 379 also included a polished aluminum hood centerline; premium UltraRide seats embroidered with the Legacy Class Edition emblem; and the Platinum Oval Package that included a punched oval-pattern grille and air cleaner intake screen, polished grille bars, and stainless-steel sun visor.

The special model also included Peterbilt's premium level interior with a ConcertClass sound system, Sirius satellite radio, and an in-dash GPS navigation system. These trucks sported the extended-hood, 127-inch BBC configuration and were available as day cabs or with Pete's full line of Unibilt sleepers.

To commemorate the company's 50th anniversary in 1989, Peterbilt released a special edition 50th anniversary Model 379, with a special logo on the sides, mud flaps, and dash plate. The trucks were painted Regent red and metallic gold just for the occasion. An anniversary model 377 was also released that year.

In late 1986, the Model 378 was introduced, which was essentially the same truck as the 379, but with a fiberglass hood. Long-time Pete aficionados say the best way to tell the two models apart is that the 378 has no rivets on the fiberglass hood.

The Model 379 set many standards, and with more than a quarter million units produced during the truck's 20-year production run, it still rules the road as the truck most desired by drivers. Their classic, long-nose profile, quality craftsmanship, and "get the job done" toughness established the Model 379 as a true long-haul legend.

Throughout the 1980s, trucks were becoming more durable, fuel efficient, and comfortable. From the mid-1980s to today, truck customers demanded more progress in these areas and Peterbilt responded by incorporating more aerodynamic designs into its lineup. Designing trucks for the new millennium required meeting even greater challenges in the areas of emission control and fuel efficiency. Trucks and the components became smarter. Computers were put on everything from engines to antilock braking systems. For-hire truckload fleets were beginning to use satellite communications systems to track and communicate with their trucks on the road. Private fleets were equipping their vehicles with on-board recorders to track engine speed, idle times, and other operational characteristics. Truck designers were prompted to incorporate many of these new developments within their models, and again, Peterbilt responded.

Chapter 5

A NEW CENTURY,
A NEW MILLENNIUM

Toward the end of the twentieth century, fuel efficiency and pollution reduction became key factors in truck design and production. More fuel-efficient and cleaner engines required different design elements, one of which was the focus on more aerodynamics. Peterbilt's models that were introduced to address these issues included the 377, 378, 357, 385, 386 (notable for the air cleaners being on the inside of the engine compartment instead of the outside like on most Petes), and the 387, an aerodynamic model that shares the same cab shell as the Kenworth T-2000.

Page 86: The 387 was introduced in 1999 to appeal to truck users who wanted an aerodynamic configuration. Long Haul Trucking runs this Model 387.

The Peterbilt 377, introduced in 1986 and produced until 2007, became Peterbilt's first aerodynamic conventional truck with a slightly sloped hood and more rounded corners than traditionally styled Peterbilts. In 1996, Peterbilt redesigned the 377 and introduced the 377 A/E, which had a sleeker, more contemporary style. The truck featured a sloped hood, streamlined headlights, and a standard chrome aerodynamic bumper.

The company introduced the Unibilt cab sleeper system in 1993. The cab and sleeper were joined to

Cliff King's 2007 Peterbilt 386 with 2006 Wabash trailer is a good example of Peterbilt's aerodynamic lineup and features a sloping hood, headlamps integrated into rounded bumpers, and roof fairings. The sleeper is a custom aftermarket product.

This pair of Peterbilt 377s went into service for Yellowstone Trucking of Coeur D'Alene, Idaho, in 1995. They featured Detroit Diesel Series 60 engines, Eaton-Fuller 10-speed transmissions, and Peterbilt's new Unibilt cab/sleeper system. *Courtesy* GO-West *archives*

form a single structure. Benefits for the driver included a 62 percent wider sleeper opening. The sleeper can be detached and the cab converted to a day cab.

Peterbilt introduced the Model 385 medium conventional Class 8 at the 1995 Mid-America Trucking Show in Louisville. The new model featured a 112-inch BBC and new set-back front axle for easier maneuverability. Company officials said the truck was well suited for inner-city and over-the-road applications. The Model 385 also featured new aerodynamic styling and a sloped fiberglass hood, the one feature that most distinguishes it from the 377. The standard engine on the 385 was the Caterpillar 3176 rated at 350 horsepower and 1,350 lb-ft of torque. Other 10- and 11-liter engines were offered as options. Antilock brakes were also standard on the 385. This model was produced from 1996 until 2007.

In March 1999, Peterbilt rolled out the Model 387 in an effort to improve its share of the aerodynamic over-the-road truck market. Aerodynamic trucks make up the lion's share of the North American Class 8 truck market. The Model 387 and other aerodynamic models would give the company the opportunity to compete in the aerodynamic market segment. During an interview at Peterbilt's Denton, Texas, headquarters in January of that year, company officials acknowledged their share of the aerodynamic market was pretty small, but they felt Peterbilt could improve in that area. Time has proven them right. The aero-style Peterbilts are popular options for fleet operations.

The new 387 offered 112- and 120-inch BBC configurations and featured a radical new design for Peterbilt, which was best known for its traditional, long-nose conventional trucks. Key to this design was a 22-degree sloped hood, chromed crown, and a stainless-steel grille design. Peterbilt said the 387 was 13 percent more aerodynamic than the 377 and 385 and comparable to other aerodynamic trucks. The 387 shared common components, such as doors, mirrors, and windows, with sister company Kenworth's T-2000, but the design was definitely unique for Peterbilt at the time.

Peterbilt created the Unibilt cab sleeper system in 1993. The key feature was the cab and sleeper joined to form a single structure. The sleeper could also be removed and the cab converted into a day cab. *Courtesy* GO-West *archives*

configurations were offered: a premium length, a high-roof, and a mid-length sleeper in both mid- and high-roof versions.

A new generation Unibilt air suspension system and tuned shock absorbers for both the cab and sleeper smoothed out the ride. The interior design featured under-dash drink holders that accommodated large mugs or cups. The drink holder on the driver's side held a 44-ounce cup. The Model 387 also included a number of design features aimed at ease of service. For instance, the hood release handle was mounted on the floor of the cab, just to the left of the driver's seat. A technician could pop the hood without climbing into the truck. Engine access was improved by the use of a two-piece fender liner. The fender liner was mounted to the hood and lifted out of the way when the hood was opened to give service technicians easier access to the engine compartment.

A single-axle Model 387 was put in service in 2003 by Taylor Made Golf to haul a pit-crew–style trailer around to PGA events where technicians set up shops, offering tune-up services to the golf professionals who use Taylor Made clubs.

Peterbilt hoped the 387 would allow the company to gain more fleet business. Peterbilt's long-haul icons, such as the Model 379, were viewed primarily as owner-operator trucks. But officials thought the truck would appeal to the segment of the owner-operator market that buys high-quality aerodynamic trucks. Company offices said at the time they had "taken the roots of the 379's heritage" to develop the new truck. The medium-length model was able to accommodate engines up to 12 liters while the 120-inch model could take engines up to 600 horsepower.

The cab and sleeper of the Model 387 were 17 percent larger than previous models. Three sleeper

The UltraSleeper, shown here on a Model 379, was introduced in 1996 and featured a full-size bed, fold-down table, and lots of storage.

The Model 386 was introduced in 2006 and was similar to the 387 but with a detachable sleeper configuration and day cab configurations. That model was used in 2007 by Peterbilt and Wal-Mart to develop a hybrid-electric truck. Peterbilt described the 386 as a combination of the 389/388 conventional model trucks and the aerodynamics of the Model 387. The 386 sported a set-back front axle for better maneuverability. The Model 384 has a shorter BBC.

Peterbilt made some slight changes in 2004, including repositioning side mirrors and eliminating the wing window to improve driver sightlines. This trend was continued in 2005 by restyling the driver- and passenger-side doors on its conventional lineup. The bottom of the window was lowered about 2 inches and angled slightly to give the driver better visibility through the passenger-side window.

Peterbilt launched a new medium-duty model in 2004 with the Model 335. The Class 6 and 7 trucks went into production in the spring of that year and featured an aerodynamic sloped hood made of composite materials that made it lightweight but durable. The truck had repeater signal lights on the quarter fenders for additional signaling capability and side air vents.

THE NEW LINEUP

Peterbilt unveiled an all-new lineup in 2006. The Mid-America Trucking Show in Louisville was once again the site of the announcement. The company described the new lineup as falling within four categories: traditional, aerodynamic, vocational, and medium duty, although many vocational and medium-duty applications overlap.

As with other product introductions during Peterbilt's storied history, the guiding design principles were quality, innovation, and versatility—Peterbilts could be specified for any job. Perhaps more important for the long-time fans of the trucks, the company also set styling right up there at the top.

The more aerodynamic Model 385 was introduced at the 1995 Mid-American Trucking Show. This truck was photographed in the Pomona, California, area in 2000.

The line was said to feature improvements in a number of areas such as aerodynamics, fuel efficiency, styling, and maneuverability. The aerodynamic line includes the Model 384 and Model 387 day cab, which along with Models 387 and 386, complete the company's aero truck lineup. The 387 day cab is targeted at tanker and regional haul applications and is available in both medium- and long-length BBC configurations.

The Model 384 can be configured as a day cab or with the full range of Unibilt sleepers. The mid-length 384 has a 116-inch BBC and set-back front axle, plus weight-saving components. A lower radiator and sloped hood improve forward visibility by almost 12 inches over previous models.

Peterbilt's traditional lineup included the Models 389 and 388, which will be discussed in more detail in the next chapter.

The new vocational models introduced in 2006 were Models 367 and 365. The 367 replaced the 357 and 358, while the 365 replaced the 111-inch-BBC Model 357. Peterbilts are configured for a variety of vocational applications. Models 340 and 330 joined Model 335 to complete the company's medium-duty truck lineup. The company introduced the Class 5 Model 325 conventional in 2007. These models are discussed in more detail in Chapter 9.

KEEPING IT CLEAN

New truck design continues to be heavily influenced by clean air and other environmental regulations. Truck makers are considering the various emission technologies needed to meet new exhaust emissions standards in 2010. Some truck makers may take a different approach than others. Engine makers may also decide to meet the new standards in different ways. That portends even more design challenges ahead.

In many states and cities, truckers are prohibited from idling their engines for more than 15 minutes, except under certain conditions. Emergency vehicles are exempt, for example. Drivers still need to be able to stay warm in the winter and cool in the summer, even with their trucks turned off. Peterbilt and other truck makers are addressing these issues with innovative new features that help truckers limit their fuel intake and idling times. The company's ComfortClass System is a no-idle system available in Peterbilt's 63- and 70-inch sleeper cabs. It includes a thermal storage system that provides a heating and cooling system and the 100-volt power to run appliances for up to 10 hours with the truck's engine turned off. The ComfortClass system's alternator charges the system's power pack and the truck's starting batteries while the truck is underway. The thermal storage unit is also charged when the engine is running. When the truck is shut off, the ComfortClass system's power pack batteries take over and run the thermal unit's fan and supply power for accessories.

The Model 378 is a popular truck for vocational applications, such as logging. It is very similar to the 379, but has a somewhat more sloped fiberglass hood.

In addition to concerns about emissions, rising fuel prices demand design changes geared toward reducing fuel consumption. In 2007, along with the new Model 389, Peterbilt began offering an aerodynamic package designed to improve the efficiency of its traditional-styled trucks. The Fuel Efficiency Package includes roof fairing; oval-shaped, cab-mounted exhaust; aerodynamic air cleaners; a contoured bumper; and other aerodynamic components. Other parts of the package include a contoured sun visor that works in combination with the roof fairing to more effectively move air over the truck.

In another move to reduce the amount of diesel fuel burned, Peterbilt delivered the first Model 386 hybrid truck to Wal-Mart stores in January 2007. Developed by Eaton Corporation, the truck's hybrid system captures energy from the engine during braking and stores the energy in a battery bank. The electrical engine from the batteries runs a motor/generator that supplies additional power to the engine's torque. The engine

A two-axle 1988 Model 378 sits outside the Las Vegas Hilton, while owner George Garcia prepares it for a truck show inside the Las Vegas Convention Center. Garcia won the first place trophy with this beauty.

Peterbilt's aerodynamic models, such as this Model 387, have become more popular fleet options and compete with other aerodynamic trucks for fleet business.

might operate only on diesel engine power, on both diesel and electrical power, or only on electrical power. The hybrid system improves efficiency between 5 and 7 percent, according to Peterbilt. Another benefit of a hybrid is that the electricity stored can also be used to power cab comfort systems, such as electric HVAC units, microwaves, and refrigerators when the driver is stopped for the night. This eliminates unnecessary truck idling. The Model 335 was also designed to use the hybrid system for stationary PTO applications.

In March 2008, Peterbilt was planning full production of Model 330 and 335 hybrid medium-duty trucks. The trucks were to be built at Peterbilt's manufacturing facility in Ste-Thérèse, Quebec.

SMART TRUCKS

Stricter emissions controls required much stricter control over what was going on inside the engine. As engine makers began creating a series to meet tougher emissions requirements in the 1990s, they found they could control emissions by more precisely controlling how much fuel was injected during combustion and when the fuel was injected in the cycle. Such control led engine makers to develop sensors that could monitor the combustion process. At the same time, federally mandated antilock braking systems required advanced sensors to monitor the system's functionality. These devices also used sensors and control modules. Other sensors could monitor tire pressure, reefer box temperatures, transmission functions, and other items.

Onboard computers were introduced to the trucking industry in the mid-1980s and private fleets began using devices to track things such as vehicle speed, engine hours, and idle time. This helped companies increase fuel mileage and reduce accidents. Some of the larger for-hire trucking fleets began using satellite systems to communicate with drivers and track their trucks. Fleets soon discovered that the GPS capability could be used to mark state-line crossings, which made it possible to automate fuel tax reporting.

Truck makers had to incorporate these new technologies into their truck designs and, again, Peterbilt proved to be up to the task. In 2001, Peterbilt unveiled an in-dash GPS navigation system for the Model 387. The Alpine DVD Vehicle Navigation System provided drivers with turn-by-turn visual and audio directions and tracked the vehicle's location and speed. Drivers just had to enter a street address or phone number and the system would provide the directions to get there. Controlled by either the touch-screen display monitor or a wireless remote, the system's capabilities included map zoom (featuring SmartMap Pro maps), detour routing, points of interest display, and a GPS clock. A new driver display introduced in 2007 was standard on Models 389, 388, 386, 384, 367, and 365. The unit is located on the dash directly in front of the driver and displays fuel economy (trip or lifetime), optimum engine speed, average speed over a measured distance, engine hours, idling hours, and truck and engine serial numbers. The display also includes warning signals that use text-based readouts instead of fault codes.

A new dash for Peterbilt's medium-duty conventional line of trucks that incorporates Peterbilt's navigation system became available in mid-2008. The system features a 5-inch VGA resolution screen with touch-screen capabilities, an MP3 audio player, and 30GB hard drive. It can provide turn-by-turn directions and visual and audio cues through the vehicle's stereo system. It comes preloaded with Peterbilt dealer locations and lodging, fuel, ATM, and restaurant locations across the United States and Canada.

MORE INTEGRATION

Peterbilts have always essentially been custom-built in the sense that customers specified the type of engine, suspension, axles, and frame length suitable for their application. In some years, truckers had a choice of three makes of engines in various displacement sizes and horsepower, transmissions from two or three different suppliers, and the same for axles, brakes, and so on.

Most heavy trucks are built to specifications, but Peterbilt has always offered an extra level of customization and specification that other truck makers did not. In Europe, ordering a truck from a "menu" of possible components is unheard of. European truck makers produce integrated products. The customer can request specific engine horsepower and displacement, axle ratings, frame lengths, and more, but only from the components offered by the truck maker.

U.S. truckers have resisted the trend toward vertical integration for years, but in recent years there has been more pressure on truck makers to limit the choices their customers have when it comes to components. Acquisitions, mergers, emissions standards, and market conditions have prompted truck makers and component suppliers to form new alliances that could change a truck buyer's choices. A move toward more integration is considered a definite trend by most industry observers, but the trend may not be all bad. Economic and competitive pressures make long-term supply agreements between truck makers and component manufacturers attractive. These deals represent a middle ground between the two manufacturing models with unlimited choice on one hand to the totally integrated European model on the other. Truck makers like these deals because they can push costs down by saving engineering costs. As new emissions standards require engine manufacturers to make difficult design choices in coming years, options for power may decrease even more.

All Dressed Up for the Show
A 379 Custom Gallery

One of the most amazing things about Peterbilt trucks is the incredible level of customization available to the truck owners. Five Model 379s that were identical when they left the factory can look like five completely different trucks within a few years. Of course, quite a few options can be added at the factory, including polished stainless steel, chrome, and air fairings. But the aftermarket is chock-full of customization products. Pete owners love their trucks and it shows. Each owner has dozens of options available from wide, square chrome bumpers to chrome sun visors and plenty of additional lights.

Jeff Botelho of Botelho Brothers Trucking in Los Banos, California, took a wrecked and burned out Peterbilt 379 and decided to build a convertible truck. He entered the truck in the Big-Rig Build-Off at the 2007 Mid-America Show and has continued to customize the truck since then. Here the truck is shown at TruckerFest in Sparks, Nevada, in August 2007.

Troy Points' 2003 Model 379 reflects the surroundings in its highly polished chrome and stainless work at the 2007 TruckerFest in Sparks, Nevada.

Owners have added special paint schemes, murals, and extra-large sleepers that are as big as some apartments. Nothing is beyond the imagination of a Peterbilt owner. Truckers who frequent the show truck circuit may lead the charge in this area, but other Pete owners get in on the action, as well.

Thomas and Kim Turner of Cynthiana, Kentucky, show their 1995 Peterbilt 379, *El Dorado*, and drop deck trailer at truck beauty shows around the country. They have put more than 800 LED lights on their truck and have added chrome wherever and whenever they can, including the steering gear and other components under the hood. Their work pays off, as they regularly win best of show and other awards at the truck shows they enter. Kim said they add things to their truck "as they go," but that they try to follow a plan as they customize their truck. A professional look is important, she said, noting that if you want your truck to look great, you don't want to overdo it. Her advice is don't start drilling holes in painted areas just to hang more lights or a piece of chrome.

At a show in Las Vegas in 2007, Sergio Gonzalez was showing his 1997 Peterbilt 379 with plenty of what he called "old school" touches. These included a rear bumper guard on the back that came from a 1953 Chevy and windows in the back of the sleeper that came from a 1951 Chevy. To continue the old school theme, he replaced the oval Peterbilt badge with an old, rectangular Peterbilt nameplate. Now that's old school.

Even a burned out Peterbilt wreck can see new life. Jeff Botelho of Botelho Brothers Trucking in Los Banos, California, rebuilt a Peterbilt that had once been a burned-out wreck. He remade it into a low-riding Peterbilt convertible with a killer sound system. The only pieces used from the original truck were the axles, frame, and parts of the cab. Everything else was fabricated, including machining down truck wheels to take sports car tires.

Here are more examples of some of the most head-turning customization jobs seen around the show circuit the last few years.

James Davis of Medford, Oregon, and his 1994 Peterbilt 379 long-hood took home some hardware from the 2007 TruckerFest in Sparks, Nevada. The judges were impressed by the paint scheme and subtle use of chrome. Note the extra-large bumper. A current trend is to outfit the truck with hydraulic controls that raise the bumper for driving and lower it to within millimeters of the ground for showing.

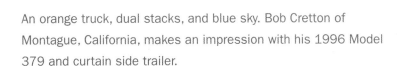

An orange truck, dual stacks, and blue sky. Bob Cretton of Montague, California, makes an impression with his 1996 Model 379 and curtain side trailer.

Gayron Hooper made a trip to the 2007 TruckerFest in Sparks, Nevada, a family affair. The truck show, which coincided with the Reno/Sparks Hot August Nights annual classic car show, included an evening cruise where the big rigs followed the four-wheelers through the streets of Sparks and Reno. The Hoopers and their 2000 Model 379 stressed a patriotic theme decked out in red, white, and blue. Ted Proudfoot, Leona Proudfoot, Diana Hopper, Gayron Hopper, and Diana Hopper are shown in the photo.

Dale and Tamara Johnson's 2007 Viper Red Pete 379 extended-hood shows plenty of chrome at the Mid-America Trucking Show in Louisville where they received an award for their use of chrome and stainless steel. Chrome shop owners say they sell more chrome for Peterbilts than just about any other truck make. The Johnsons' combination is strong evidence of that fact.

Above and opposite page: Randy and Jona Rebillard of Gimli, Manitoba, are truck beauty show veterans and have won frequently with their 2002 Peterbilt 379, *Tired Iron*. The truck features some interesting customization, including an old-style Peterbilt nameplate, a paint scheme depicting rusting rivets, and an interesting hood ornament.

Thomas and Kim Turner are regulars at truck show events and compete with their immaculate 1995 Model 379 and matching Transcraft step deck trailer. At last count, the Turners had more than 800 lights on their combination. The customization doesn't stop with the exterior, as shown by this photo of the engine compartment in full show dress. Note the chrome (which includes the steering gear and other components), polished hoses, and leather sleeves. The truck's name is even painted on the engine.

Sergio Gonzales operates SG & Sons Trucking in San Diego and showed his 1997 Peterbilt 379 at the 2006 Stars & Stripes Truck Beauty Show in Las Vegas. Sons, German, Sergio Jr., and Sebastian helped their dad at the show. The truck features what Gonzales called old school touches, such as rear bumper guards from a 1953 Chevy, sleeper windows from a 1951 Chevy, and the old school rectangular Peterbilt nameplate. "Now that's real old school there," he says. The neat touches include old-style single headlights, a two-tone paint scheme, and suicide doors that open from the front.

Chapter 6
THE NEW FLAGSHIP: MODEL 389

The Model 389 became Peterbilt's standard bearer in 2007 when the last Model 379 rolled off the company's Denton, Texas, assembly line. Following a legend such as the Model 379 is no small feat, but Peterbilt believes the 389 is up to the task. It combines the traditional style of the Model 379 with improved aerodynamics, lighter-weight construction, and other technological innovations designed to help reduce fuel consumption and decrease operating costs. At first glance, one would be hard pressed to tell the difference between the Model 389 and

Page 110: The Model 389 retains the traditional Peterbilt look, despite a number of updated systems and components.

its predecessor, and that is what Peterbilt engineers had in mind.

The Model 379 was not retired because it wasn't popular. That truck was in as high demand as ever as both new and used. It was the increasingly tougher federal emissions standards that went into effect in 2007 and the even more strict standards planned for 2010 that brought the end to the 379. The new standards meant that engine makers had to make drastic changes to their powerplants to accommodate cleaner engines. The newer engines required increased cooling from the trucks' cooling systems, and higher capacity radiators and improved airflow under the hood were essential.

Peterbilt engineers did not want to change too much. In fact, in terms of parts and components, the Model 389 is virtually identical to the Model 379, with a few key exceptions. The 131-inch BBC and new hood are certainly different. The interior is upgraded and there are a few other styling differences that distinguish the 389 from its predecessor, but other than that, the new model is a chip off the old block in every way and may prove to be an even more desirable ride.

At the truck's introduction in 2006, Dan Sobic, then general manager of Peterbilt, addressed the new engine

This brand-new Model 389 was being prepared for service by technicians at Teresi Trucking in Lodi, California. A headache/storage rack is attached behind the cab, and the rear is modified for hauling low-boy and drop-deck loads.

The very modern-looking headlights are among the most noticeable differences between the Model 389 and its predecessor, the Model 379.

requirements and noted fuel efficiency was something engineers paid close attention to when designing the Model 389. Better aerodynamic performance has never been an issue with Peterbilt buyers. After all, they want a large car. They prefer their trucks to have that long, tall traditional hood. The trucks' continued high resale value speaks volumes about the demand for Peterbilts. With diesel fuel prices soaring over recent years, better fuel economy has also become a concern of even the most diehard traditional truck customers.

Among the design features aimed at increasing fuel economy is a new lightweight-aluminum hood that includes Peterbilt's anti-blowdown feature to prevent the hood from accidentally closing. The new all-aluminum hoods were designed to be durable and lightweight with superior fit and finish. The truck also features a one-piece aluminum surround with a punched-oval pattern grille, polished-aluminum

grille bars, new headlamps, and an aerodynamic hood ornament. The air cleaner screens also have the punched-oval pattern.

The grille surround is a one-piece unit and one of the visible differences between the 389 and 379. As a one-piece unit, the grille surround lacks the seams and rivets of the Model 379's grille surround, giving it a cleaner appearance. The edges are also more rounded, as are the corners. Another noticeable difference between the 379 and 389 is the aero-dynamic headlamps on the 389. These lamps use halogen low-beam projector and high-beam complex-reflector lights to increase forward lighting and improve bulb life. Peterbilt says the new lamps put off double the light of the previous models and the bulbs last up to 60 percent longer. Long-life LED directional signals are integrated into the headlamps. The headlamp pod is made of aluminum with an impact-resistant lens cover. Aero-style mirrors help reduce drag by as much as 40 percent over previous designs, states Peterbilt. An added bonus of the new mirrors is better rearward visibility.

An optional Fuel Efficiency Package, available for both the Model 389 and shorter wheelbase Model 388, includes a contoured sun visor and roof fairing; oval-shaped, cab-mounted exhaust; aerodynamic air cleaners; streamlined tool and battery boxes that have rounded front edges to smooth airflow; a contoured bumper; and underbody fairing. Peterbilt says this package can reduce fuel consumption about 3/10 of a mile per gallon.

The Model 389 also features improved wheel cut for better maneuverability and a 90-degree tilt hood for easier access to service points. Simplified routings in the chassis provide easier access to service points, and new, lighter-weight cooling system features increase cooling capacity to accommodate higher horsepower engines. The cooling system also has a new fan shroud design and silicon hoses.

The Model 389 retains the traditional Peterbilt look, despite a number of updated systems and components.

The 389 features a more aerodynamic hood ornament, which is one of several touches designed to make the truck more fuel efficient.

The Model 389 is available in two cab configurations, low roof or UltraCab, and three trim levels. The Peterbilt GPS navigation system comes standard with the premium Platinum-level trim. The dash-mounted GPS system delivers turn-by-turn voice instructions for finding addresses. All a driver has to do is punch in an address or a telephone number and the system provides hassle-free driving instructions. The GPS navigation system also has an MP3 player and is tied into the truck's audio system.

Like all the previous Peterbilts, the Model 389 is a versatile truck. It can be specified as a day cab or sleeper in either a Unibilt or Unibilt UltraCab configuration. Sleepers are available in lengths of 36, 48, 63, and 70 inches and are available in two trim levels. Depending upon the configuration, the sleepers can include a number of closet and cabinet options and bunk configurations. A bunk-side panel controls the lights, HVAC system, stereo, and optional equipment, including a refrigerator/freezer. The panel also includes a digital alarm clock.

The 389 can be specified for a number of applications with axle and suspension ratings to match just about any job, whether that is on-highway or off-road. Peterbilt offers six frame rail and wheelbase options for extra versatility. Whether pulling a refrigerated trailer down the interstate or hauling rocks and dirt in a dump body, the 389 and 388 are up to the job. The

The Model 389 boasts a number of aerodynamic features, including rounded edges and air foils, but it still maintains the traditional Peterbilt long-nosed and broad-shouldered look.

The Model 389 features the Unibilt system for a seamless cab and sleeper configuration. The sleeper compartment can be removed and the truck converted to a day tractor.

truck can be specified in single-drive, single-drive with tax axle, tandem-drive, or tridem-drive configurations with 15-liter engine options from Caterpillar C15 or Cummins ISX of up to 600 horsepower. The transmissions available are a 9-, 10-, 11-, 13-, 15-, or 18-speed Fuller manual; 10- or 18-speed Fuller Autoshift; or a 10- or 13-speed Fuller Ultrashift.

As mentioned earlier, the 388 is the same truck but with a shorter hood. The Model 388's BBC comes in at 123 inches, which Peterbilt calls the mid-length hood. The 388 can accommodate 15-liter or 13-liter engines.

The new models retain all the well-known Peterbilt manufacturing touches, such as building the aluminum cabs with huck-bolted, lap-seamed construction and bulkhead-style doors for a durable, watertight and rattle-free structure.

Chapter 7

VOCATIONAL MODELS

While many people think classic, long-nosed highway trucks when they think about Peterbilts, the company's heritage is in work trucks. Peterbilt built its reputation for making durable, tough work trucks decades before the long-road was a reality. That stellar reputation was forged in the woods, mines, oil fields, quarries, and construction sites throughout the Pacific Coast and other parts of the West.

The first Peterbilts were work trucks, and the work truck tradition has continued through the years with Petes found in most vocational applications imaginable. From cement mixers to off-highway oil field trucks, Peterbilts have always delivered the goods on the work site. Some operators, such as ready mix fleets, may run their Peterbilt mixer trucks for 20 years or more before replacing them. Of course, due to the nature of the load—concrete that must be delivered from the plant to a job site within a fairly short time period—mixer trucks don't usually rack up many miles each year. The trucks still take a beating as they are often required to operate at construction sites or other off-highway locations. Getting 20 years of work out of a truck is the very definition of value and durability.

The wide range of choices truck buyers have in specifying their Peterbilt trucks makes each vehicle essentially custom-built with plenty of options for

Page 118: This 1996 Model 379 transfer dump shows the versatility of this model as it is can be used as a highway tractor, dump truck, off-road truck, to name a few. This truck is operated by Teresi Trucking in Lodi, Calif.

frames, engines, transmissions, axles, and other components. That's why two different Peterbilt Model 379s may look alike, but underneath they are completely different trucks.

When the company first began building trucks, Peterbilt used three serial number prefixes to designate the type of truck it was: S for small, L for large, and M for chassis only. The company later began using different

This and opposite pages: Just because you work in the dirt and rocks all day long doesn't mean your truck can't look good. Michael Blakeslee of Wolcott, Connecticut, works his 2002 Peterbilt dump truck every single day, but he keeps it looking great with plenty of custom chrome touches.

serial numbers and added prefixes to the numbers to indicate an all-aluminum frame (A), aluminum frame with steel crossmembers (M), and an all-steel frame (S or ST). Off-road and vocational trucks tended to have the S or ST designations because more steel means more strength. With the introduction of its new product lineup in 2006, Peterbilt began listing its trucks in four model classifications: traditional, aero, vocational, and medium-duty.

At an event for Peterbilt construction customers in Tucson, Arizona, a few years ago, a company engineering manager noted that "Peterbilt has always remained true to its heritage, having begun in off-road applications. And those heavy-duty, sturdy trucks helped build the Peterbilt legend."

Most of Peterbilt's models through the years, with the exception perhaps of some cab-over models, have been used in vocational work. In recent years, Model 378 and 379 heavy-haul tractors with 46,000-pound rear axles have rolled off of Peterbilt's assembly line, along with Model 379 transfer dumps and Model 385 bulk haul trucks, to prove the brand's well-known versatility. Models such as the 360 and 381, on the other hand, were brutes suited for rugged off-road work rather than on-highway hauling.

The Model 353, a direct descendant of the 351, was designed for construction work. The Model 348, with a sloping fiberglass hood, was introduced in 1970 as suitable for dump truck work. The Model 357 was a standard truck for construction, super dump, and other heavy applications. Peterbilts are also popular in mixer applications. In recent years, Peterbilt has controlled about 16 to 18 percent of the mixer market. Models still working on job sites across the country include the 357, 362, 379, 385, 387, and 330.

Other notable Peterbilt vocational trucks include Models 370, 380, and 390, which were introduced in the late 1940s and early 1950s. These trucks did not

This Model 357 SBFA conventional was capable of hauling 10 yards when it went into service for Florida Mining and Materials in 1992. Its specifications included a 119-inch BBC, 205-inch wheelbase, Rockwell RF21-155, 21,000-pound front axle, Rockwell RT46160, 46,000-pound rear axle, 13 3/8-inch steel rail frame, 260-horsepower Cummins L10 engine, 10-speed Eaton-Fuller RTO-11708LL transmission, and super-single Michelin 445/65R22.5 radial tires. One of the trucks was exhibited at a 1993 Truck Maintenance Council meeting on the benefits of super-single tires. *Courtesy GO-West archives*

have skirted fenders and were built for heavy-duty work, such as logging. The 370 featured a steel bar attached to the bumper to protect the radiator and a distinctive wooden platform on the roof where a worker could stand during loading and unloading operations. The Model 380 looked similar to the 370, but it had a wheelbase that was about 4 inches shorter on the base model. The Model 390, built from 1949 until 1953, was another logging truck similar to the 370 and 380 but with a 197 1/4-inch wheelbase on the base model.

The Model 381, a heavy-duty off-road truck introduced in 1954, found great acceptance in construction, mining, aggregate, and dump truck applications. It was built of all steel, including the cab, and included double- or triple-frame construction when the operating conditions demanded the necessary reinforcements. The Model 381's fenders were wide, square-shaped, and flat on the top. A walkway that ran from the rear of the fender to the rear of the cab provided additional space for workers while loading and unloading material. The Model 381 was a long-nosed truck with a BBC that measured more than 135 inches.

Peterbilt's classic Model 359, introduced in 1967, made its reputation as an over-the-road truck, but it could be specified for all kinds of work, including dump and mixer applications. Its classic good looks and legendary durability made it popular with construction, mining, and other companies that wanted a truck that could handle the hard work with ease but look good doing it.

The Model 341, also introduced in the 1960s, was designed for mixer and dump applications and became an instant success. With a 113-inch BBC and front bumper extension for power take-off, it proved to be

continued on page 128

Peterbilt double-dump rigs have been a common site on Western highways for more than 50 years.

Restoring Old Trucks

As seen in a number of the photos presented in this book, many Peterbilts from the 1940s and 1950s have been restored to their original luster, if not their original configuration. According to Darrow Thomson, Jr., owner of the Courtland TruckWorks in Courtland, California, these restorations often involved significant fabrication work because the parts are no longer available. The Courtland TruckWorks started as a truck repair shop about 12 years ago, and the workers spend most of their time restoring old Peterbilt trucks. "We started out doing truck repair for the farmers around here and we began working on an old Pete when we had time," Thomson says. "Gradually, we started doing more, and now this accounts for about 80 percent of our business."

In addition to doing restoration, Courtland TruckWorks sells hoods, fenders, cab panels, and other parts to collectors doing their own restoration projects. These parts are fabricated on site, since that's the only way they can get them. Thomson says the first thing they had to make was the rubber for the windshield. "We could get a windshield made, but we didn't know where we could get the rubber seals." They also began making hoods, fenders, and other sheetmetal. Thomson said most of the old trucks they work on are pretty well rusted out, and most of the time, the only thing that can be salvaged from the cab is the original frame. The company sells a lot of hoods, especially the butterfly-type hood.

A ground-up restoration may take as long as a year, depending upon the condition of the original truck. Thomson says the company has microfilm files of the Peterbilt build records from the earliest days up into the late 1970s. "A lot of guys will call and say, 'I just bought this old truck and have a serial number. What can

Peterbilt cabs sporting names of old trucking companies are stacked outside the shop at Courtland TruckWorks in Courtland, California. Owner Darrow Thomson says the cabs for many Peterbilt models are very similar. "They used the same cab for a number of models," he says.

you tell me about it?' They like to know when it was built, who bought it, and things like that," he says.

But knowing the original equipment list doesn't mean that his customers want the truck restored to exact original specifications. "Let's face it," Thomson says. "It's not fun to drive the old-style truck. So the first things most guys want are an updated powertrain, power steering, air conditioning, air-ride, and updated electronics. They want to be able to drive it, hook it up to a trailer, and enjoy it."

The company has quite a collection of old Peterbilts and parts, with cabs stacked three-high behind the work shop, old trucks lined up two deep out front, and another lot of old trucks stored in another yard. These old trucks provide parts for restorations or cores for a new restoration. On the sides are the names of trucking companies that have faded from memory, but one doubts these old trucks will follow. Even though they are worn out and rusted, the old trucks still look like they could be on the road again with a little TLC.

Peterbilts from the 1940s and early 1950s sit in a garage at Courtland TruckWorks where they will either serve as a core or provide parts for a restoration project. It can take a year or more to get trucks like these to look as they did when they were running the highways.

This 1952 Peterbilt awaits eventual restoration but had not seen active service for some time. Moss was growing on the hood and rust has had its way with most of the sheet metal, which is a common condition on most of the old trucks the Courtland TruckWorks technicians work on. The truck had seen some modifications over the years with the addition of an extra horn and a roof-mounted air conditioning unit.

Peterbilt work trucks exhibit a bold, tough look, as if they are ready for anything. In most cases, they are.

continued from page 123

the perfect truck for these applications and allowed Peterbilt to garner a sizeable piece of the mixer and dump markets they still enjoy today.

The 1960s also saw the arrival of the Model 383, an off-highway truck designed for the toughest applications. The long-nosed 383 (BBC was 140 inches) featured a standard gross volume weight of 83,000 pounds and a gross commercial volume weight of 150,000 pounds, which is enough truck for the hardiest of applications. The frame was extra tough and made with heat-treated alloy steel with all the parts bolted together for extra strength. The cab was all-steel and instead of rounded fenders, the 383 used flat fenders made of steel with a walk-on surface. The

Peterbilt's Model 365 is said to be ideally suited for dump and mixer or other heavy-use applications.

Great paint and the right amount of chrome make this dump and transfer trailer rig look great. This truck was at the Petro Truck Stop in Sparks, Nevada, during the 2003 TruckerFest.

383 did not have a platform on the cab roof, nor did it have a side platform running on the side of the cab underneath the doors.

In 1972, Peterbilt rolled out the Model 353, which was a heavy-duty version of the 359. The Model 353 had a long, butterfly-style hood and sported a BBC dimension of 177 1/4 inches. The fenders were heavy-duty, flat-topped steel with a safety walk anti-skid surface. The standard rear suspension was built for heavy work and rated at 55,000 pounds.

A tandem front-axle Model 353 was also built that featured a severe-service cab with all-steel back panels, roof panels, and windshield mask. The hood of this particular model had steel slide-in sides for engine access and flat steel fenders with the anti-skid surface.

Another off-road truck was the Model 387, which was built from 1975 to 1982. Its heat-treated, 110,000-psi

frame and severe-service steel-cab construction made it one tough truck. A 350-horsepower Cummins Big Cam II engine provided the power and Rockwell 65,000-pound rear axles carried the load. For very heavy loads, axle ratings up to 28,000 pounds in the front and 150,000 pounds in the rear were offered. The truck has a 54 3/4-inch setback axle, flat steel fenders, and an anti-skid walking surface.

The Model 357 became the company's signature work truck when it was unveiled in 1986. The standard model featured a slightly sloped, fiberglass hood with a 111-inch BBC and fiberglass fenders. To accommodate set-back or set-forward front axle configuration, optional BBCs of 119 and 123 inches were also available on the Model 357. The 123-inch BBC model had a butterfly-type steel hood. Standard power was supplied by a 285-horsepower Caterpillar 3306B, with optional engines up to 444 horsepower available from Cummins and up to 425 horsepower from Caterpillar. The truck could be specified with a variety of severe-service options, such as flat steel fenders and heavier front and rear axles. A 6x6 drive configuration delivered power to all six wheel positions for handling tough off-highway conditions.

At the 2006 product introduction, Peterbilt unveiled Models 367 and 365 as the basis of its vocational line, which also includes Models 340 and 320. The 367 replaced the 357 and 358, while the 365 replaced the shorter-hood 357 models.

Available in set-forward and set-back axle configurations, the 367 was designed to be suitable for any job. These models feature a lightweight but durable composite hood with Peterbilt's hood opening mechanism. The Model 367 has a 124-inch BBC and is used in logging, refuse, dump, and construction work. Available as a day cab or with a low-roof Unibilt sleeper, the 367 can haul bulk or other heavy over-the-road work. Front or rear power take-off options are available. The Model 367 is also offered in a special heavy-haul configuration with a larger cooling system and heavy-haul hood. The 115-inch BBC Model 365 can be specified with various engine, axle, and suspension options to handle a variety of loads. This truck is also offered with Peterbilt's transit mixer and transfer dump packages, which makes them construction work ready. For over-the-road operations, the 365 can handle the 36-, 48-, and 63-inch low-roof Unibilt sleepers.

Both the 367 and 365 trucks feature high-performance headlamps that are protected by a durable aluminum housing. Peterbilt's ProBilt interior package is designed for vocational work, but the higher-level Platinum and Prestige interior trim packages are also available.

While Peterbilt classifies the Model 340 as a medium-duty truck, it is used in a variety of vocational applications, such as dump, crane, refuse, and bulk delivery operations. The truck features a number of heavy-duty components and can be specified with either single- or tandem-drive rear axles. A number of options are available that make the 340 suitable for a number of construction work jobs.

All lined up and ready to go, this team of Petes was at the Ability First Working Truck Show in Pomona, California, during June 2000.

Anywhere you find construction trucks gathered, such as at these mixers, you are bound to find Peterbilts like these two.

Pete's aerodynamic Model 386 and Model 384 day cabs are also popular choices with many vocational customers in truck and tractor configurations. The 384 day cab is a 116-inch BBC truck with a set-back front axle that can be specified with heavy-duty components for all types of vocational work. Engines from 280 to 485 horsepower and Fuller manual or Ultrashift transmissions are available. The Model 386 day cab has a 126-inch set-back front axle and can be specified with engines up to 600 horsepower.

In recent years, more vocational customers have specified automatic transmissions. Peterbilt offers a range of automatic and semi-automatic transmissions on a number of its models. Lightweight, heavy-duty suspensions, such as Hendrickson's HaulMaxx, can add payload in a number of vocational applications. The HaulMaxx was introduced on Peterbilt trucks in 2001 and was exclusive to Peterbilt and sister truck maker Kenworth. The HaulMaxx was about 700 pounds lighter than other vocational suspensions.

In addition to building trucks for vocational applications, such as construction, logging, bulk-hauling, off-road, and other vocational work, Peterbilt focused on other niches, such as refuse. Peterbilt started building trucks designed for refuse work in the 1970s, and started with the CB300. The truck was made in Montreal for both Peterbilt and Kenworth. The Model 310 followed in 1978, and the Model 320 replaced the 310 in 1987. Peterbilts were some of the first refuse trucks in which the driver could drive the truck while standing on the right side.

The 320 features a 96-inch-wide cab and an interior designed with ergonomics in mind, which makes it a comfortable low-cab-forward truck. The cab can be configured for right-hand, left-hand, or dual-position drive. The right-hand drive configuration can be made to operate while standing up. For added safety, the 320 comes pre-wired for backup or other positional cameras, which have proved to be popular in many refuse applications due to the frequent reversing required in this kind of work.

A Model 378 tri-axle dump truck with a pusher axle takes on a load of dirt during a demonstration at the Caterpillar Proving Grounds in Tucson, Arizona, in 2001. The event showcased Peterbilt's vocational lineup.

A 111-inch BBC Model 357 with a reliance dump body works out in the dirt during a Peterbilt/Caterpillar vocational demonstration held in Tucson, Arizona, 2001.

Frame liners can be specified for heavier applications, and the truck is available with power take-off options. The Model 320 has proven to be a reliable performer and was still manufactured in 2008.

The Model 320 has found its place in other applications besides refuse. In one example, it proved to be just the right fit for an agricultural trucking operation based near Salinas, California. Until about 2000, Rapid Harvest was using 30- to 40-year-old harvesting trucks that had been manufactured by the FABCO Manufacturing Company between 1956 and 1981. The trucks had a wide track and were especially designed for use in harvesting crops, such as lettuce and other produce.

While FABCO had exited the specialty truck-building business, it remained in the axle and transfer case business and one of its customers happened to be Peterbilt. Rapid Harvest repowered, reaxled, reinforced, patched, and fixed the old FABCO trucks until they couldn't be fixed anymore. Finally, the FABCO trucks were replaced with Model 320 flatbeds with a 33,000-pound gross volume weight, a six-wheel-drive configuration, a 164-inch wheelbase, and a 180-inch track so the super single tires fit perfectly between the rows of crops. Two prototypes were put in service in 2002 and the results were great. Rapid Harvest added more Peterbilts to its fleet of lettuce trucks. From lettuce to trash, for more than 60 years Peterbilts have proven they can handle just about any job that comes their way.

Chapter 8

MEDIUM-DUTY TRUCKS READY FOR WORK

Peterbilts have always been known as heavy-duty trucks that today would be classified as Class 7 (26,001 to 33,000 pounds) and Class 8 (over 33,001 pounds). The Model 334 was rated at 42,000 pounds; the Model 260 was rated at either 32,000 pounds or 37,000 pounds, depending upon the specifications; and the Model 280 was rated at 26,300 and 36,000 pounds. All would have been considered Class 8 trucks by today's standards. Because they were custom-made trucks, Peterbilts could be specified with heavier or lighter weight components to fit

Page 134: This Model 335 is outfitted with a crane truck body for service and construction work. Peterbilt medium-duty trucks feature streamlined hoods and fenders with integrated headlight assemblies.

other weight ranges, but for the most part, the company built heavy trucks. The standard Model CB 200 low-cab-forward model sold in the 1970s was rated at 31,000 pounds gross volume weight (GVW), which made it a Class 7.

According to U.S. Census figures, there were about 2.6 million Class 8 and Class 7 trucks in use in the United States during 2002. There were another 900,000 Class 6 medium trucks and about 1.9 million trucks classified as Classes 3 to 5. The census defines heavy trucks as those in Class 7 and 8. Class 6 trucks are defined as light-heavy, while medium trucks are defined as those in Classes 3 through 5. Light trucks are those less than 10,000 pounds GVW in Classes 1 and 2 and represent pickups, SUVs, minivans, and regular vans.

The markets for trucks in the Class 3 (10,001 to 14,000 pounds GVW) to Class 6 (19,501 to 26,000 pounds GVW) range are quite a bit different from Peterbilt's traditional market of vocational and over-the-road trucks. While a number of medium trucks are used in construction and other vocational applications, many more are used in businesses that do not have anything to do with trucking, with the exception that they use trucks. To put it another way, a typical over-the-road for-hire trucking company uses the trucks it owns to generate revenue: Shippers pay these companies to move freight from point A to point B. Private fleets, on the other hand, use their trucks as tools in their primary business. They are typically carrying their own goods. Think of the large discount retailers or grocery chains that operate large over-the-road truck fleets. No

one is paying them to move their own groceries from a distribution center to a store.

Most medium-duty truck users operate private fleets. The trucks are not revenue generators but tools these companies use in their day-to-day business. Medium-duty truck users include cities and counties, utilities, bakers, appliance stores, lumber yards, furniture stores, plumbers, HVAC contractors, nursery operators, local delivery firms, beverage distributors, and construction firms. Their trucks are delivery trucks, walk-in vans, landscape trucks, bucket trucks, cranes, beverage trucks, rack trucks, stake bodies, and flat beds, to name a few. You will find heavy trucks in many of these fleets, as well, but it's a benefit for a company if it can use medium-duty trucks rather than a Class 7 or 8 truck. Drivers operating trucks under 26,000 pounds GVW are not required to hold a commercial driver's license (CDL) unless they are operating a bus that carries 10 or more passengers or hauling hazardous materials that require placarding.

Few U.S. truck makers try to offer products for every market segment in every weight class. Some European automotive companies do and offer vehicles ranging from automobiles to heavy commercial trucks. U.S. companies that had once manufactured everything from cars to Class 8 over-the-road trucks cut back on the types of vehicles offered (GMC) or got out of the heavy truck manufacturing business altogether (Ford). Heavy truck makers in the United States have traditionally left the lower classes to others. In recent years, however, most U.S.-based Class 8 truck makers have branched out to new markets and are offering trucks in weight ranges as low as Class 5 and 6.

For some years, the products offered in the medium segment were limited with few options for a company that needs something bigger than a 1-ton pickup but didn't need a Class 6 or Class 7 truck. European and Asian truck makers, such as Iveco, Renault, Isuzu,

Peterbilt medium-duty trucks are used in a number of applications, such as utility or other work, where aerial lifts are required.

The Model 335 can be specified as either a Class 6 or Class 7 truck, which makes it suitable for many vocational applications, such as car hauling, light mixer work, and other jobs.

Mitsubishi, and others, began selling Class 3, and Class 4, low-cab-over trucks in the 1980s to meet a demand for smaller, city delivery vehicles and service trucks. Truck makers began offering more choices between Class 2 and Class 7 as the demand for these products continued to rise. Rising gasoline prices prompted many to investigate alternatives to the gasoline-powered pickup chassis cab configuration. Operators who had been using gasoline-powered Class 3 or Class 4 trucks found that diesel power could

The Model 220 low-cab-forward medium-duty truck is based on the DAF LF, which is made by DAF Trucks, a commercial truck maker based in Europe and owned by Peterbilt's parent, PACCAR. The DAF was named the 2006 European Truck of the Year.

save them money in the long run because of better fuel economy and reliability. While most U.S.-based heavy truck makers have not extended their product ranges into the lower range of medium trucks, they have addressed Classes 5 and 6.

For a number of years, many segments of the medium-duty market were considered price driven. In other words, when buying trucks, these companies were mostly interested in how much the trucks cost. Discussions of life cycle costs, driver comfort, durability, and other factors important to heavy truck

fleets were not considered to be as relevant to these companies. Most believed they wanted to buy the least amount of truck they could to get the job done.

This view of the market held a premium truck built by a heavy truck maker, such as Peterbilt, a disadvantage. But Peterbilt saw plenty of opportunity for its products in markets besides long-haul and heavy vocational work. Time has proven it right. While purchase cost is still a major consideration for most medium-duty truck buyers, durability, quality, and overall life cycle costs are also

A Model 330 with a stake bed body is a Class 6 truck that can be used in applications where drivers don't require a commercial driver license.

important considerations, and Peterbilt believes its products offer buyers greater value in these areas. Even for those applications that don't put a lot of stress on the truck, using a brand such as Peterbilt makes a statement about the company that runs

them. That is why today, Peterbilts can be found in all types of medium-duty truck fleets.

Peterbilt began offering more medium-duty models in the late 1990s, and today the company offers a full range of medium-duty trucks from Class 5 (16,001 to 19,500 pounds GVW) through Class 7 trucks. Today, Peterbilt's medium-duty lineup is also well represented in the vocational market, with the 335, 330, 320, and 220 seeing plenty of work in dump and construction applications.

Introduced in 2007, the Model 325 is a Class 5 conventional vehicle designed for a number of applications, such as vehicle recovery and towing, P&D, construction, truck rental/leasing, landscaping, or similar services. Rated at 19,500 pounds GVW, it featured a PACCAR PX-6 engine with horsepower ratings from 200 to 300 horsepower. A six-speed manual is standard with an automatic transmission available as an option. The 325 comes standard with front and

A fiberglass hood and headlamps that are integrated into the aerodynamic fenders give Peterbilt medium-duty trucks a distinctive look that's noticeably different from the company's traditional models.

rear hydraulic disc brakes and an anti-locking brake system. It features an all-aluminum cab, steel bumper, and composite hood and fenders. Like its big brothers, the 335 has a stainless-steel grille with a chrome surround.

The Model 335 can be specified as either a Class 6 or 7 vehicle. Peterbilt says the truck is a good fit for applications such as pickup and delivery, beverage distribution, municipal use, refuse, and fire and rescue. The 335 is a Class 7 truck used in van body, beverage, or other medium-duty work. Engine choices include the PACCAR PX-6 or PACCAR PX-8 engine.

The Model 220 and Model 210 are medium-duty Class 7 and 6 cab-overs, respectively, that are used in a variety of applications. Both trucks are available in non-CDL configurations. Both of these models were introduced in 2006 and are based on the DAF LF, made by DAF Trucks, a commercial trucker based in Europe that is also owned by Peterbilt's parent company, PACCAR. The DAF LF was named International Truck of the Year by European truck journalists in 2006. These new models are part of a growing trend. Many truck makers are part of multinational corporations. Peterbilt's parent, PACCAR, isn't the only U.S. truck maker with ties to truck makers based outside the United States. Mack Trucks is part of Sweden-based Volvo Trucks. Freightliner, Sterling, and Western Star belong to Germany-based Daimler. While not all truck designs from Europe or elsewhere will be suitable for the U.S. market, some clearly are, especially in the lower weight classes.

The company's latest medium-duty models, the Model 330 and Model 340, extend the company's versatile lineup even further. These two models, along with the 325, are built at PACCAR's Ste-Thérèse, Quebec, manufacturing facility.

The 340 is built for heavier Class 7 and lighter Class 8 (known as a Baby 8) uses, such as dump truck applications. The Model 340 has a 33,000-pound GVW and can be specified with heavy-duty options like double-frame rails, high-capacity axles (up to 46,000-pound capacity rear axles), and frame extensions for front or rear power take-off. The standard engine for the Model 340 is a PACCAR PX-8 at ratings from 240 to 330 horsepower. Peterbilt says this model is also suited for other vocations, as well as for municipal applications.

The lightweight Model 330 is a Class 6 configuration that is available with GVW ratings up to 26,000 pounds. It can be equipped with hydraulic brakes and low-profile tires to allow for operation by non-CDL drivers, which is a huge benefit for companies in that it enlarges the pool of potential drivers. Standard power is the PACCAR PX-6 engine with horsepower ratings from 200 to 323.

Chapter 9
PETERBILT CAB-OVERS

Peterbilt has been building cab-over-engine trucks since the early 1950s. Pete's predecessor company, Fageol Motor Car, had built cab-over models. Engineering drawings from the early 1940s show Peterbilt's interest in cab-over trucks. Today, cab-over trucks represent a small percentage of the heavy truck market. According to a U.S. Census Bureau report on truck inventory and use in 2002, cab-over models accounted for only about 11 percent of all Class 7 and 8 trucks and an even smaller percentage of Class 6 trucks. Most of those trucks are involved in vocational work.

Page 142: A Model 362, one of Peterbilt's most popular cab-overs, hauls cattle trailers as part of the Valley Enterprises fleet.

Conventional trucks are by far the most preferred style in the U.S. market and throughout North America. The United States' trucking industry expanded along with the roads that were built to link growing towns and cities together. When state and federal transportation officials planned the interstate highway system, they understood these new highways needed to be wide enough for heavy trucks. The exact opposite is true in

This picture and the one accompanying it show Peterbilt cab-overs on Highway 50 in early 1992. At one time, cab-over tractor trailer configurations were the most common seen on the road. The 1982 elimination of overall length limits on federal highways and other routes in the national network allowed trucks to pull long trailers with longer conventional trucks. Within 20 years, most truck makers were no longer building cab-overs for the over-the-road truck market.

Europe where cab-over trucks have dominated. Space constraints and strict length regulations have made a conventional truck all but extinct in most of Europe.

The conventional or cab-over question has been going on since the earliest days of trucking. A review of a motor truck exposition that ran in the January 21, 1912, edition of the *New York Times* noted that "Many of the wagons had the driver's seat above the motor. The driver's seat behind the motor, as in pleasure cars, appears to be the most favored," even though the opinion of most attending the exposition was that, "from every point of view it is better to mount the driver above the motor." History has not reflected this preference, at least not in the case of over-the-road highway trucks. In that category, cab-overs represent a small percentage of the Class 8 truck market. There are still 603,000 cab-overs in service, according the Census Bureau report. Cab-overs are perfect for a number of applications where maneuverability and space are an issue. They are prominent in urban delivery fleets and are by far the most common type of truck used for garbage hauling, recycling, and other municipal services.

There was a time when cab-overs were the most popular truck configuration sold. This popularity stemmed from a number of factors. For one thing, without a long nose in front, maneuverability was better with a cab-over. Some drivers found the cabs to be cozy, and since there was no hood to obstruct their view, drivers also appreciated the better visibility cab-overs offered. Since the driver is sitting right on top of the bumper, the view of the road directly in front of the truck is superb. That's not the same for a conventional truck, especially for those with exceptionally long noses. For instance, in the 131-inch BBC Model 389, a driver can't see anything on the ground in front of the truck unless it is more than 30 feet in front of the bumper.

The most important factor in the popularity of cab-overs were length laws. For a number of years,

A Model 362 straight truck was photographed at the Petro truck stop in Sparks, Nevada, during the 2003 TruckerFest. Because of their maneuverability, the models are often used to deliver building materials to urban job sites and suburban subdivisions with narrow streets.

tractor-trailer combinations were restricted to a 55-foot length limit on U.S. highways and in many states. If truckers wanted to haul longer trailers in order to carry more cargo with each load, cab-overs fit the bill.

The age of the cab-over, at least in the United States, saw the beginning of the end when Congress passed the Surface Transportation Act of 1982, which abolished overall length limits, among other things. Trailer limits were instituted with 53-foot trailers now being the maximum length allowed on most roads. Some states and municipal jurisdictions continue to enforce length laws on state and local roads. In some states, there is no overall length limit for tractor-trailer combinations, but such limits exist for truck and full-trailer combinations or tractor and multiple-trailer combinations. Because of these state rules, cab-overs are still used in some areas, but for the most part that style of truck has fallen out of favor with truck drivers and fleets. By 1986, conventional trucks were the most popular configuration on the highways.

While the cab-overs had several sterling qualities, they could not compete with conventional trucks in a number of areas. Drivers believed they had a smoother ride in a conventional truck, and conventionals are more ergonomically friendly in terms of ingress and egress. Getting into a cab-over is not easy. Drivers have to maneuver themselves over the front wheel and into the cab via steps and grab handles. By contrast, getting into a conventional truck is a simple climb up a few steps. Because conventional truck cabs sit behind the engine, there wasn't as much of a "doghouse" [room]

Hay haulers are among the truckers that still use cab-over trucks. This 1994 Pete is owned by Mike Maggini of Riverdale, California.

This 1953 Model 350 cab-over sports a similar grille design as the conventional 350 with vertical shutters and a crossbar.

This 1953 Model 350 cab-over cattle hauler, or at least the frame and running gear, was the first truck Ed Rocha bought when he branched out from his father's company and started his own business. Rocha used the truck for a number of years and sold it. He found it some years later, minus the original cab. Rocha replaced the cab and restored the old truck.

This is the interior of a 1954 280 cab-over owned by Ed Rocha of Rocha Valley Enterprises in Oakdale, California. It's fairly Spartan by today's standards and is dominated by the Ross steering wheel.

This is a 1954 Model 280 cab-over hooked up to two cattle trailers from the same period. It's essentially the same as the Model 350, but with a single drive instead of dual drive.

in the cab as with a cab-over, although recent truck designs of both configurations have moved to flat-floor-type cabs.

Cab-over cabs lent themselves to integrated sleeper compartments. The sleeper and cab could be built in one unit to provide more interior space and an easier pass through from the driver's seat to the bunk. This design was also developed for conventional models so that the roomiest sleepers are found on today's conventional trucks.

All these changes meant that by the end of the twentieth century, with the exception of a few brief resurgences, most heavy truck companies quit building cab-over models for long-haul trucking. Peterbilt stopped building its last cab-over model, the Model 362, in 2005. The company still manufactures low-cab-forward models for various vocational markets, especially refuse.

The gear levers in early Peterbilt cab-overs extended somewhat horizontally from the rear cab, as shown in this 1954 Model 280.

PETE CAB-OVERS: A SHORT HISTORY

Peterbilt made some special-order cab-over versions of its models from the earliest days. It offered production cab-overs beginning in the 1950s, with the COE versions of Models 280 and 350 in 1950 through 1959, and Models 282 and 352, which were built from 1959 all the way through 1980.

To get into the cab of this Model 350 cab-over, a driver or passenger had to make sure to start the climb with the correct foot placed in the stirrup step. Note the no-skid surfaces on the cab side and fender.

A 2000 Model 362, operated by Jade Transport of Winnipeg, Manitoba, Canada, was among the contestants at the 2007 Mid-America Trucking Show's Paul K. Young Memorial Truck Beauty Show.

In a brochure for its Model 280 and 380 cab-overs, Peterbilt trumpeted them as "a modern answer to increased pay loads," and noted that length and weight limits presented truckers with a huge challenge in running a profitable trucking company.

The trucks were designed to allow carriers using the short-wheelbase trucks to haul longer trailers within a given length and increase their payload capacity. These trucks were the bubble nose–type of cab-over and not the flat-faced models that came in later years. The headlights were mounted inside the front panel. In addition, the trucks were designed to allow easy access to the engine and front axle components. The fenders swung up, which allowed technicians to easily check fluids and to access components, such as the steering gear, air compressor, fuel pump, and fuel filter. The front panel also swung open, which allowed access to the air cleaner, headlights, radiator, electrical circuits, and the fuel, oil, and air lines. For complete access to the engine, the whole cab tilted forward 90 degrees and was held in place by steel cables. With the cab tilted, mechanics could work on or remove the engine or the whole powertrain. The transmission, clutch, and other components could be serviced via the fender openings. A small dog house extended into the cab to just between the driver and passenger seats. The transmission levers on these models extended from between the seats from a position behind the driver in an almost horizontal orientation.

The dual-drive 350 was available in wheelbase lengths of 135 to 190 inches. The single-axle 280 cab-over had wheelbases of 111 to 194 inches. With the introduction of the Model 281 and 351 cab-overs in 1955, Peterbilt unveiled the Panoramic Safe-T-Cab design, with a flat-front similar to the front that all later cab-overs featured. The cab came in a regular or sleeper configuration with a two-piece wraparound windshield that gave it a Safe-T-View. The sleeper could also be positioned above the driver to allow for a longer trailer. The bunk, or sleeping compartment, folded to the rear when not in use and was a very cozy or tight space, depending upon how one views small spaces. When the sleeping compartment was down, the passenger seat folded forward to allow room as the sleeper cab was only 9 inches longer than the standard cab.

For the single-drive-axle 281 cab-over, wheelbases from 105 to 152 inches were available. The dual-drive 351 cab-over was available on wheelbases of 141 to 173

inches. As with all Peterbilts, various transmission, axle, and engine choices were available to accommodate a range of applications.

Peterbilt made Model 451 and 356 cab-overs in 1956 and 1957 for one of its customers. These trucks featured a flat engine with the sleeper compartment on top. The 451 also had dual front axles and dual rear axles, while the 356 was a three-axle truck. This design did not catch on and only about 60 of these trucks were manufactured.

The Model 282 and 352 cab-overs were produced between 1959 and 1980 and were quite popular with long-haul truckers. BBC dimensions of 54, 63, 73, and 86 inches were offered to accommodate various sleeper arrangements. These models were quite common on the highway and came standard with a

Peterbilt only built the Model 372 from 1988 to 1993. It was Peterbilt's most aerodynamically styled cab-over, but was introduced at a time the cab-over was losing favor among North American truckers. This 1989 372 was operated by Brian Tank of Remington, Indiana.

Are they unloading air cargo from plane to truck, or loading air cargo from truck to plane? Whatever the case may be, Ringsby Truck Lines of Denver, Colorado, is on the scene for the move. The Peterbilt you see here is a Model 451 that was made in 1956 and 1957 for Ringsby. The engine was a pancake Cummins that was mounted below the frame rails. The original cab had the sleeper on top of the cab, but those cabs were removed and fitted with a conventional engine and the Model 351 sleeper cab like we see here. The axles were twin steering. The Dromedary body was made by Strick. These units ran from Denver to Salt Lake City, and then to either San Francisco or Los Angeles. There were 39 of these units produced. *Ron Adams Collection*

250-horsepower Cummins NHC-250 engine, Fuller 15-speed transmission with overdrive, Rockwell axles, a 63-inch tilting cab, and a cooling system that featured horizontal radiator shutters.

The Model 352 86H, introduced in 1976, was an 86-inch BBC truck that could also be specified with a 110-inch cab to accommodate a large sleeper compartment. The key difference between this model and the previous Model 352 cab-over was a larger radiator that allowed the trucks to be equipped with larger, higher horsepower engines. To accommodate the larger radiator, the cab height

The Model 352 was introduced in 1959. The first ones had the narrow bumper. The new model went to the dual headlights from the singles on the previous 351. This 352 is set up as a livestock truck-trailer combination. The cab measures only about 50 inches. The short cab allowed the hauler to carry a few extra head of cattle for more payload. *Ron Adams Collection*

International Transport Inc., of Rochester, Minnesota, was a nationwide heavy hauler. Its fleet was made up of owner-operators who had a different variety of brand-name tractors. In this case we have an early 1960s Model 352. This one has a 73-inch cab. Part of the load is a Cleveland Model V140, and what looks to be a ditch digger. Notice all the license plates. They were part of the necessary dress code back in those years. *Neil Sherff*

The Model 352 had a face lift in 1968. The new look was the dual headlights in a recessed square. This change made for a better appearance. This 352 was owned by Clyde Harrington who was in the East-West Division, based in Omaha, Nebraska, for Refrigerated Transport Inc., based in Atlanta, Georgia. The cargo box is a Timpte reefer trailer. *Harry Patterson*

was raised about 4 1/2 inches, as measured from the top of the frame rail.

The Model 362 replaced the Model 352 as Peterbilt's signature cab-over truck and was introduced in 1981 and produced until 2005. The truck had a 90-inch sleeper cab, but optional BBC measurements of 54, 63, 82, and 110 inches were also available. The 54-inch cab was not a sleeper. The standard model came with a 300-horsepower Cummins NTC 300 Big Cam engine, Fuller Roadranger nine-speed transmission,

Another Model 352 is this one owned by T. B. Ball, Jr., of Sanford, Florida, that is hooked up to a Great Dane reefer trailer. This was the typical 352 with the exception of the sun visor and the four headlight shields.
Neil Sherff

Rockwell axles that were 12,000 pounds in front, and a 38,000 tandem in the back. Optional power choices included Caterpillars up to 450 horsepower, Cummins up to 600 horsepower, and Detroit Diesel up to 425 horsepower. Engine choices depended upon the cab

BBC. Heavy-duty versions and tandem-steer versions were also available. The 362D and 362F were a 63-inch BBC nonsleeper cab version (D) and a 90-inch BBC sleeper cab version (F) of the 362. Even though cab-overs started to wane as the over-the-road truck of

The Model 352 was found in all types of hauling. Here we have another moving company, and this time it is Bekins Moving & Storage Co. A good number of moving rigs had a Dromedary body behind the cab. This one has the 86-inch cab. *Harry Patterson*

The Model 352 was the kind of tractor that was involved in pulling all kinds of loads and trailers. Here we see one pulling a set of Fruehauf doubles. By the early 1970s, Peterbilt started to offer the bigger bumpers. The owner was Child Truck Line. *Ron Adams Collection*

choice within a few years of the truck's introduction, the Model 362 had a successful run.

In 1995, Peterbilt introduced Model 362E, an enhanced version of the Model 362 cab-over. It was prominently displayed at the 1995 International Trucking Show in Las Vegas, Nevada. The 362E was lighter than previous 362s and went into production during the third quarter of 1995. It was available in 90- and 110-inch BBC configurations. The cab was 5 inches lower and had deeper and longer steps to ease in and out of the cab. It was among the first

cab-overs to offer Peterbilt's Classic III interior, which until then had been available only in the company's conventional-model trucks.

The Model 372, an aggressively aerodynamic cab-over model, was built from 1988 to 1993. Some said the Model 372 looked like a motor home and it was widely known by the nickname *The Football Helmet*. The 372 featured a 108-inch BBC. The cab used a hydraulic system to tilt 63 degrees for engine access. The cab and sleeper were constructed of aluminum and fiberglass and featured a roof fairing and cab side extenders for improved aerodynamic performance. The front corners were noticeably rounded, which added to the truck's ability to easily slice through the wind.

The engines available for the 372 included a Caterpillar 3406 rated up to 425 horsepower, a Cummins NTC Series with up to 444 horsepower, and a Detroit Diesel Series 60 with up to 400 horsepower. A 315-horsepower Cummins was the standard engine. A wide selection of Fuller and Spicer transmissions were offered with the 372 with a nine-speed Fuller Roadranger gearbox as standard equipment.

Peterbilt quit building the Model 372 in 1993 and the last Model 362 rolled off the assembly line in 2005. Most other heavy truck makers also quit making

In 1973, Peterbilt joined the ranks of the other two western truck makers by introducing its new double bunk cab-over engine. The new cab measured 110 inches, which was 2 inches longer than the VIT Kenworth and 6 inches longer than the White-Freightliner Vanliner. The engine for this was an 8V-92 TA Detroit Diesel turning out 430 horsepower. The transmission was a Fuller 13-speed. The rig was owned by Marlin Smith of Fort Pierce, Florida. *Harry Patterson*

At first glance, you might think this tractor is a Kenworth, but look again. It is a 352 110-inch big cab Peterbilt. What is misleading is the flaring along the bottom of the cab and the paint design. Otherwise, it is all Peterbilt. The company it works for is Tri-State Motor Transit Inc. of Joplin, Missouri, which is a heavy hauling carrier of government and military equipment. *Harry Patterson*

cab-overs for over-the-road and other freight operations. Cab-overs or low-cab-forward models are now mostly used for refuse, sanitation, and other work.

While the cab-over lost favor among over-the-road truckers, low-cab-forward designs are widely used in a number of vocational markets, especially in refuse and sanitation work. The Model 320, technically a low-cab-forward truck, was introduced in 1985 and was used extensively in refuse and related work. Peterbilt redesigned the 320 in 1995, and the new model offered improved driver comfort by raising the hood and straightening the back of the cab. These changes increased head and belly room for the driver.

The 320 is suitable for a number of applications, including agriculture. Rapid Harvest of Salinas,

California, uses Peterbilt Model 320s as harvesting trucks. Rapid Harvest began replacing its FABCO harvesting trucks, many of which were 40 years old, in 2003. The 320s are specified as three-axle, all-wheel-drive trucks with single tires all the way around that must operate within the tight confines of vegetable fields.

Peterbilt introduced the Model 220 low-cab-forward medium-duty truck in 2006. The Model 220 is based on the DAF LF, introduced by DAF in 2001. DAF, a European truck manufacturer, is also owned by Peterbilt's parent company, PACCAR. The truck was first offered in a Class 7 configuration, but in late 2007, the truck was offered in a Class 6 configuration.

Index